INQUIRING MAN:
The Psychology of Personal Constructs

INQUIRING MAN:
The Psychology of
Personal Constructs
THIRD EDITION

Don Bannister
and
Fay Fransella

ROUTLEDGE
London and New York

First edition published 1971
by Croom Helm Ltd
Second edition published 1980
by Penguin Books Ltd
Third edition published 1986
by Croom Helm Ltd
Reprinted 1987

Reprinted 1989
by Routledge
11 New Fetter Lane
London EC4P 4EE

© 1986 Don Bannister and Fay Fransella

Printed and bound in Great Britain
by Biddles Ltd, Guildford and King's Lynn

Library of Congress Cataloging in Publication Data

Bannister, D. (Donald)
   Inquiring man.

   Bibliography: p.
   Includes indexes.
   1. Personal construct theory. I. Fransella, Fay.
II. Title. [DNLM: 1. Personality. 2. Psychology.
BF 698 B216i]
BF 698.B3143   1986   155.2   84-22410

ISBN 0-415-03460-4

CONTENTS

PREFACE

Successive prefaces to new editions of a book give the authors increasing confidence in the book's relevance (since people are continuing to read it) but they also challenge them to make clear their developing purposes in preparing these new editions.

Our preface to the first edition of *Inquiring Man* introduced the book as an attempt to make clear what was singular about Kelly's theory of personal constructs. That purpose remains and we still strive 'to emphasise that construct theory sees man not as an infantile savage, nor as a just-cleverer-than-the-average-rat, nor as the victim of his biography, but as an inveterate inquirer, self invented and shaped, sometimes wonderfully and sometimes disastrously, by the direction of his enquiries'.

Our preface to the second edition stressed the way in which personal construct theory was being taken up by a wide range of professional groups and applied to a diversity of fields 'as varied as architecture, anthropology, religion, literature, commune life, map construction, body image, language, children's notions of self, delinquency and deviancy, teaching techniques, methods of group psychotherapy, liking and disliking, depression, social skills, racial identity and so on and so forth'. This is now more than ever true and we could add to our original sampling of fields, areas such as economics, history, computerised learning, mental handicap, aphasia, vocational guidance and many others.

This third edition can serve an additional purpose because it comes on the scene a full thirty years after Kelly's publication of his theory in *The Psychology of Personal Constructs*. In that thirty years, while the theory has acquired proven status as a practical tool and as a rich source of new thinking, traditional psychology itself has undergone vital, if cautious, change. The Behaviourist view of persons as docile organisms, totally shaped by their environment, has yielded ground over the last thirty years, to the tide of 'cognitive psychology'. Psychologists have, with great effort, reached an obvious conclusion in their labours — if psychologists can think then it may be that their subject matter (people) can think. Psychologists are edging towards a more humanistic vision of persons as active and creative, as agents in their own right, not simply as responders to stimuli.

However, while the development of cognitive psychology has begun to resolve the paradoxes that bedevilled early mechanical man models, it is raising fearsome problems of its own; some so baffling to the new wave in psychology that they have been simply ignored. These problems are precisely those upon which personal construct theory might cast light. Thus any cognitive psychology (by definition) accepts the ancient division of the person into 'cognition' and 'emotion' (thought and feeling, reason and passion and all such traditional dichotomies). Since cognitive psychologists are puzzled as to how these two might relate, they informally agree to carve up the person and arrive at non-competing (because separate) *psychologies* of cognition and emotion. We are left with the unrelated homunculi of thought and feeling.

Personal construct theory provides an integrated view of the person by seeing 'emotion' as neither more nor less than construing in transition. Thus the person is seen as a unity within a unified psychology. Equally, cognitive psychology is trapped by the rigid nature of its instruments (formal psychological tests) and by its lack of developed theory, into working in terms of the conventional segments of 'cognition', functions such as 'memory' and 'perception' or areas such as 'number' or 'language'. Kelly, by providing more imaginative ways of exploring our construing (repertory grid method and self characterisation) and by developing a view of our constructs as hierarchical and patterned into sub-systems, liberated psychology from what he called 'the dread disease of hardening of the categories'.

In the next decade, personal construct theory may well continue to be seen as radical, unorthodox and challenging, yet it may also begin to be seen as relevant to the problems and themes of current psychology, to be seen as speaking to the same issues, rather than be regarded as an outsider.

When a scientist propounds a theory he has two choices: he can claim that what he says has been dictated to him by the real nature of things, or he can take sole responsibility for what he says and claim only that he has offered one man's hopeful construction of the realities of nature. In the first instance he makes a claim to objectivity on behalf of his theory, the scientist's equivalent of the claim to infallibility. In the second instance he offers only a hope that he may have hit upon some partial truth that may serve as a clue to inventing something better and he invites others to follow this clue to see what they can make of it. In this latter instance he does not hold up his theoretical proposal to be judged so much in terms of whether it is the truth at last or not — for he assumes from the outset that ultimate truth is not so readily at hand — but to be judged in terms of whether his proposition seems to lead toward and give way to fresh propositions; propositions which, in turn, may be more true than anything else has been thus far. (Kelly, 1969, pp. 66-7)

Currently many psychologists feel that psychology should concern itself more with 'whole' people. It should centre more on 'real human experience'. This is comical in one sense — it is as if sailors suddenly decided they ought to take an interest in ships — but necessary in another. A variety of vanities have caused psychologists to turn their backs on the complete and purposeful person. A craving to be seen, above all, as scientists has led them to favour the clockwork doll, the chemical interaction or the environmentally imprisoned rat as their models of humanity. Further decades of massive production by psychologists has left us still open to Notcutt's accusation:

Scientism is to science as the Pharisee is to the man of God. In the psychology of scientism there is everything to impress the onlooker — enormous libraries, and a systematic search of the journals, expensive instruments of exquisite precision and shining brass, complicated formulas, multi-dimensional geometries and differential equations, long strange words of Greek origin, freshly minted enormous calculating machines and white coated girls to punch them — all the equipment is there to make the psychologist feel that he is being really scientific — everything in fact except ideas and results. Full many a glorious thesis have I seen wending its dignified way to a trivial and predestined inconclusion, armed *cap-à-pie* with all the trappings of scientism; the decimals correct, the references in order, only the mind lacking. (Notcutt, 1953, p.4)

It seems that once a profession of 'psychologists' was established it was deemed necessary to find ways of viewing people which would maintain a decent trade union differential between the professional psychologist and his object of study, the 'organism'.

Nothing So Practical As A Good Theory

In every scientific discipline, bar psychology, workers seem to accept the idea that their science will advance in terms of elaborating and testing theories. In psychology many of us behave as if 'theory' were like heaven — a fine place to go to when the practical business of living is all over, but not a matter of much concern here and now. We manifest our contempt for theory by using the word indiscriminately. We devalue it by referring to little assemblies of concepts, notions such as 'cognitive dissonance', 'reversal theory', 'catastrophe theory', and so forth.

The term 'theory' should be reserved for extensive and elaborated systems of ideas cast in terms of an integrated language. Users should not have to borrow, in every intellectual emergency, from elsewhere and conclude by assembling a ragbag of concepts which cannot be cross-related. It should be reserved for such formalised structures of ideas as have a wide *range of convenience* so that they may ultimately explain much that is not even envisaged at the time they are constructed. Yet always the explanation must be derivable from, and relatable to, what has gone before.

A theory is not a dogma

A common objection to theories stems from the belief that they are limiting, blinkering and imprisoning devices. This belief confuses theory with dogma. A dogma is something that it is proposed we live by — a scientific theory is something that it is proposed we live with and explore. In the case of dogma we may cherish and defend it, in the case of a scientific theory we should cherish and attack it. Scientific theories must be regarded as expendable; they are designed to be tested to the limit. Far from blinkering they should liberate in the sense that they formulate new issues for us to consider, new pathways for us to explore — issues and pathways which would not be available to us had not the theory pointed out their existence.

The kind of psychologist who sees theory as enslavement usually sees empiricism and eclecticism as kinds of freedom. But the near-mindless collection of data and its promiscuous attachment to whatever stray concepts happen to be around in times of need, is not freedom. It is a lack of point and direction. On this issue of theory and freedom Kelly said:

> Theories are the thinking of men who seek freedom amid swirling events. The theories comprise prior assumptions about certain realms of these events. To the extent that the events may, from these prior assumptions, be construed, predicted and their relative courses charted, men may exercise control, and gain freedom for themselves in the process. (Kelly, 1955, p. 22)

Characteristics of the Psychology of Personal Constructs

There are several respects in which personal construct psychology may seem strange to those encountering it for the first time.

Presentation

Firstly, it is presented as a complete, formally stated theory. This is very unusual in psychology, where theories tend to be stalactitic growths, which have accumulated over the years (often with later accumulations contradicting earlier ones). It would be a brave and foolish person who said they knew exactly what 'learning theory' was or what 'Freudian theory' was. Construct theory was put forward as a complete and formal statement by one man at one time (Kelly, 1955). Although experiments, arguments and inter-pretations have built up around the theory, it is still possible to state its central tenets in an orderly fashion.

Reflexivity

Secondly, the theory is reflexive. Personal construct theory is an act of construing which is accounted for by personal construct theory. Putting it another way, it does not, like learning theory, account for all kinds of human behaviour *except* the formulation of learning theory. Construct theory treats scientists as persons and persons as scientists. One of the effects of this is to make the model person of personal construct psychology look recognisably like you: that is, unless you are the very modest kind of person who sees themselves as the stimulus-jerked puppet of learning theory, the primitive infant of psychoanalytic theory or the perambulating telephone exchange of information theory. If you do not recognise yourself at any point in personal construct psychology, you have discovered a major defect in it and are entitled to be suspicious of its claims.

Level of abstraction

Thirdly, construct theory was deliberately stated in very abstract terms to avoid, as far as possible, the limitations of a particular time and culture. It is an attempt to build a theory with a very wide range of convenience, a theory not tied to one particular concept-phenomenon. It is not a theory of 'learning', of 'interpersonal relationshps', of 'development', of 'perception'. It is certainly not a 'cognitive' theory, although many textbooks have tried to categorise it as such, perhaps because the authors could not comprehend the shocking idea that Kelly did not want to use, at all, the construct of cognition *versus* emotion (Bannister, 1977, Mancuso and Hunter, 1983).

It is a theory which attempts to redefine psychology as a psychology of persons. At first reading, the theory often seems dry because it is deliberately content-free. It is the user of the theory who has to supply a content of which the theory might make sense. Kelly had particular terrains which concerned him, such as the understanding of psychotherapy, but he sought to make his psychology comprehensive enough to serve the purposes of those with very different issues in mind.

Philosophical assumptions

Finally, the theory does not have its philosophical assumptions buried deep inside it, it has them explicitly stated. Kelly gave the label *constructive alternativism* to these philosophical assumptions and argued them at some length. At one point he summarises them thus:

> Like other theories, the psychology of personal constructs is the implementation of a philosophical assumption. In this case the assumption is that whatever nature may be, or howsoever the quest for truth will turn out in the end, the events we face today are subject to as great a variety of constructions as our wits will enable us to contrive. This is not to say that one construction is as good as any other, nor is it to deny that at some infinite point in time human vision will behold reality out to the utmost reaches of existence. But it does remind us that all our present perceptions are open to question and reconsideration and it does broadly suggest that even the most obvious occurrences of everyday life might appear utterly transformed if we were inventive enough to construe them differently.
>
> This philosophical position we have called *constructive alternativism*, and its implications keep cropping up in the psychology of personal constructs. It can be contrasted with the prevalent epistemological assumptions of *accumulative fragmentalism*, which is that truth is collected piece by piece. While constructive alternativism does not argue against the collection of information, neither does it measure the truth by the size of the collection. Indeed it leads one to regard a large accumulation of facts as an open invitation to some far-reaching reconstruction which will reduce them to a mass of trivialities.
>
> A person who spends a great deal of his time hoarding facts is not likely to be happy at the prospect of seeing them converted into rubbish. He is more likely to want them bound and preserved, a memorial to his personal achievement. A scientist, for example, who thinks this way, and especially a psychologist who does so, depends upon his facts to furnish the ultimate proof of his propositions. With these shining nuggets of truth in his grasp it seems unnecessary for him to take responsibility for the conclusions he claims they thrust upon him. To suggest to him at this point that further human reconstruction can com-

pletely alter the appearance of the precious fragments he has accumulated, as well as the direction of their arguments, is to threaten his scientific conclusions, his philosophical position, and even his moral security. No wonder, then, that, in the eyes of such a conservatively minded person, our assumption that all facts are subject — are wholly subject — to alternative constructions looms up as culpably subjective and dangerously subversive to the scientific establishment. (Kelly, 1970, pp. 1-2)

Kelly is here asserting that we cannot contact an interpretation-free reality directly. We can only make assumptions about what reality is and then proceed to find out how useful or useless these assumptions are. This is a popular contention in modern philosophy and many psychologists pay at least lip-service to it. However, in much psychological writing there is a tendency to revert to the notion of a reality whose nature can be clearly identified. Hence the use of the term 'variable' as in the phrase 'variables such as intelligence must be taken into account'. 'Intelligence' is a dimension which we have invented and in terms of which we construe others. It is not a *thing* which *must* be taken into account. Entirely different constructions can be used which do not involve such a dimension at all. In our schooldays we recognised constructive alternativism when we wrote our history essays in terms of the *political, religious* and *social* aspects of a particular period. However, even then there was a tendency to talk about political, religious and social 'events' as if these were really separate events, rather than various ways of construing the same events.

Free will versus determination

This approach has implications for the great *free will* versus *determinism* debate. One is that *free-determined* is a way we construe acts and it is useful only to the extent that it discriminates *between* acts. To say that one is entirely determined is as meaningless as to say that one is entirely free. The construction (like all interpretations) is useful only as a distinction and the distinction must have a specific range of convenience. A person is free *with respect* to something and determined *with respect* to something else. In this way construct psychology avoids the determinist argument that puts the arguer in the paradoxical position of being a puppet *deciding* that he is a puppet. How many scientists, who say that they are determinists, sound like determinists when they are describing the glories of scientific method? They extol a deliberate manipulation of the universe in order to explore (note the teleology) its nature. Equally, construct theory avoids the doctrine of unlimited free will which suggests a humanity that cannot be understood because it has no 'cause and effect' aspects. In contrasting this approach with that of Freudians (you are the victim of your infancy) and behaviourists (you are the victim of your reinforcement schedules), Kelly argued that you are not the victim of your autobiography though you may *enslave yourself* by adhering to an unalterable view of what your biography means. Thereby you may fixate your present.

From this same standpoint Kelly rejects 'hydraulic' theories of humanity — theories which postulate some 'force' (motive, instinct, drive) within persons, impelling them to movement. He argues that it is entirely unnecessary to account for movement in a theory which makes movement its central assumption. Thus he says:

> Suppose we began by assuming that the fundamental thing about life is that it goes on. It isn't that something *makes* you go on; the going on *is the thing itself*. It isn't that motives *make* a man come alert and do things; his alertness is an aspect of his very being. (Kelly, 1962, p. 85)

In the light of this approach we see that Kelly is not proposing personal construct psychology as a contradiction of other psychologies, but as an alternative to them — an alternative which does not deny the 'truths' of other theories, but which may provide more interesting, more inspiring, more useful and more elaborate 'truths'.

The Formal Structure of Personal Construct Theory

The theory is formally stated as a fundamental postulate and eleven corollaries (Mancuso and Adams-Webber, 1982).

Fundamental postulate: *A person's processes are psychologically channelised by the ways in which they anticipate events.*

This implies many things. It implies that you are not reacting to the past so much as reaching out for the future; it implies that you check how much sense you have made of the world by seeing how well that 'sense' enables you to anticipate it; it implies that your personality is the way you go about making sense of the world. The word 'anticipates' is deliberately chosen because it links the idea of prediction with the idea of reaching out and beating the world to the punch. Our joyful successes and terrifying failures in anticipating the future are vividly illustrated in Kelly's (1978) essay 'Confusion and the clock'.

This fundamental postulate is Kelly's attempt to state what a person is in business for. Other psychological theories have assumed that a person is in business to process information or to adapt to the environment or to reduce drives or to obtain wish fulfilment. Kelly stresses that a person is in business to understand their own nature and the nature of the world and to test that understanding in terms of how it guides them and enables them to see into the immediate and long-term future. Thus the model person of construct theory is 'the scientist'. In saying that all persons are scientists Kelly is clearly not saying that we all wear white coats, use jargon or fiddle with test tubes; he is saying that we have our own view of the world (our theory), our own expectations of what will happen in given situations (our hypotheses) and that our behaviour is our continual experiment with life. For Kelly science has the same central characteristic as art —imagination.

This fundamental postulate is Kelly's answer to the age-old argument of whether it is nature or nurture that determines our life, whether we are controlled by our environment or living in terms of our personality. A personal construct psychology answer would be that we are reacting to our environment *as we see it*, or, to put the same thing the other way around, we are working out our own nature in terms of a real external world. Our purposes and issues are our own, but they can only be furthered to the degree and in the way that we understand external reality.

This picture of us as striving for *personal meaning* is elaborated in the following corollaries.

Construction corollary: *A person anticipates events by construing their replications.*

The dinner we ate yesterday is not the same dinner that we ate today, but our use of the construct *dinner* is an explicit recognition of some sameness, some replication, which we wish to affirm. Thus, underlying our making sense of our world and of our lives, is our continual detection of repeated themes, our categorising of these themes and our segmenting of our world in terms of them.

Kelly used the analogy of listening to music to illustrate this corollary, because it allowed him to stress that the replication is something which emerges because of our interpretation. Each time we hear a melody played in a piece of music, different instruments may be used, there may be a change of key, there may be a change of rhythm and so forth, but we still recognise the replicated melodic theme. At a very basic level the themes we recognise, the sameness we detect, can be concrete, as in our noting new examples daily of *pencils* and *sneezes* and *motorways*. Or they may be very complex, subtle and highly abstract re-plications, as when we recognise that once again we have met *defeat*, experienced *beauty* or spoken *the truth*. Be it noted that these replications *may* have verbal labels attached to them or *may* be experienced *non-verbally*, for constructs are the discriminations we make, *not* the labels we attach to them.

Kelly is here aiming to make every assumption clear, to reach down to the obvious which must be stated if a theory is to be built up in an explicit manner. Thus, our capacity to recognise re-plicated themes is also an explicit assumption of the traditional idea of conditioning. Yet behaviourist psychologists miss the essentially personal nature of the transaction they call conditioning because they give the status of reality to the generally recognised replications on which they base their experiments. For example, we might attempt to condition a subject to give an eyeblink res-ponse to the stimulus *prime number* by blowing a puff of air into the eye of the subject every time a prime number is flashed on a screen, but not when a non-prime number is flashed on the screen. Whether we succeed in establishing such a conditioned response will depend on whether the construct *prime number* versus *non-prime number* exists in the personal construct system of our sub-ject. If it does not they might condition to replications that they *can* perceive. For example, the experimenter might establish a conditioned response to odd numbers (providing the subject can construe *odd numbers*) though the experiment would then have become an intermittent reinforcement study. Yet no matter how many conditioning trials the subject is given, a *new* prime number will not necessarily elicit the conditioned response. The pre-sentation of the same prime number many times might establish a conditioned response to that particular number but not the re-plicated theme of *primeness*.

The fallacy of stimulus-response psychology (and its more

sophisticated derivatives) lies in the belief that a person responds to a stimulus. No one ever yet responded to a stimulus. They respond to *what they interpret the stimulus to be* and this in turn is a function of the kind of constructions the person has imposed upon the universe. Thus, Humphrey (1933) pointed out that you can condition (by electric shock) a person to withdraw their arm when the note G is played on the piano, but when you play them 'Home Sweet Home' they will not twitch a muscle, although the tune contains the note G 14 times — presumably because they construe it as a 'tune' and not as a series of notes.

Individuality corollary: *Persons differ from each other in their construction of events*.

It could be argued that the fundamental mystery of human psychology is covered by the question 'Why is it that two people in exactly the same situation behave in different ways?' The answer is of course that they are not in the 'same' situation. Each of us sees our situation through the 'goggles' of our personal construct system. We differ from others in how we perceive and interpret a situation, what we consider important about it, what we consider its implications, the degree to which it is clear or obscure, threatening or promising, sought after or forced upon us. The situation of the two people who are behaving differently is only 'the same' from the point of view of a third person looking at it through their own personal construct goggles.

Among the many implications of this statement is that when people are said to be similar, it is not necessarily because they have had the same experiences, but because they have placed the *same interpretations* on the experiences they have had. Two bank clerks may work at adjoining counters and live what are, in objective terms, very 'similar' lives, but they may be entirely unable to make sense out of each other. Yet one of the bank clerks may well be corresponding with an aged missionary working out his or her life's significance in the jungles of some tropical country. The bank clerk and the missionary may find their exchange of letters full of mutual understanding, because they have basic similarities in their ways of construing events. This corollary does not argue that people never resemble each other in their construing (the later sociality and commonality corollaries cover this), but it does argue that, in the final analysis, none of us is likely to be a carbon copy of another. Each of us lives in what is ultimately a unique world, because it is uniquely interpreted and thereby uniquely experienced.

Organisation corollary: *Each person characteristically evolves, for their convenience in anticipating events, a construction system embracing ordinal relationships between constructs.*

The term 'system' in the phrase 'a personal construct system' directly implies that a person's constructs are interrelated. In this corollary Kelly is stressing that the relationship is often one of inclusion, of subsuming. For some people the construct *traditional jazz* versus *modern jazz* may be subsumed as a subordinate implication of the construct *good jazz* versus *bad jazz* and both poles of the construct might be subsumed under the 'music' end of the construct *music* versus *noise*. This hierarchical quality of construct systems is what makes our world a manageable place for us. The simple trick of grouping hundreds of different ways of making a living under the construct *jobs* (versus *hobbies* or versus *rest* or versus *vocations*) means that we can then easily handle a whole range of such subordinate constructions. We can offer them to each other, look at their higher, more superordinate implications, add to the category when necessary and so forth. A further way of regarding this corollary and evaluating it is given in the following terms:

This pyramidal structure of construct systems seems to serve a variety of purposes in science and in living. For example, if we accept that the more superordinate constructs will have more implications and a wider range of convenience than their subordinate constructs, then 'climbing up our system' may be a way of finding strategies for cross-referring more subordinate constructions which cannot be directly related to each other 'across' the system. Thus the old adage that you can't add *horses* and *cows* is nonsense as soon as you climb up the sub-system and subsume them both as *farm animals* and you can blithely add in *hermit crabs* if you are prepared to climb up as far as *forms of organic life*.

Equally you may use the hierarchy as a conflict resolving process by taking decisions in terms of the most superordinate, relevant construct. For example, for some of us *courteous-discourteous* may be a subordinate construct to *kind-unkind* and if this is so, we may in exceptional circumstances decide to be *discourteous* if we feel that in the long run this is the *kindest* way to be (say in curtailing a mutually disastrous relationship). However, if that is the way we organize our constructs, then it would not make sense for us to be *cruel* in order to be *courteous*. Going down the pyramid: if we assume that for us *spitting in the spittoon-spitting on the carpet* is a subordinate construction (one possible operational definition if you like) of the construct *courteous-discourteous* then again, in exceptional circumstances (say in a culture which has reversed our particular rituals), we may find it makes sense to *spit on the carpet* in order to be *courteous*. (Bannister, 1970, p. 57)

Dichotomy corollary: *A person's construction system is composed of a finite number of dichotomous constructs.*

Kelly is here arguing that it is more useful to see constructs as having two poles, a pole of affirmation and a negative pole, rather than see them as concepts or categories of a unipolar type. In line with his philosophy of constructive alternativism he is not asserting that constructs *are* bipolar and that they are *not* unipolar. He is asserting that we might find it more useful to think about them *as if* they were bipolar. Most people recognise bipolarity where it is explicitly labelled — *black* versus *white, up* versus *down, nice* versus *nasty, concrete* versus *abstract.*

However, Kelly asserts that even where there is no label readily available for the contrast, we never affirm without implicitly denying, *within a context.* There would be little point in asserting that 'I am tired' if the contrast assertion of freshness and energy were not implicitly around somewhere to be negated. When we point and say 'That is a chrysanthemum', we are not distinguishing it from every other object in the universe, we are usually contrasting it with some other flower with which it might have been confused. This is what we are doing *psychologically*, whatever the logicians say we are doing *logically*.

The idea of bipolarity in constructs also allows us to envisage a variety of relationships between them — they can be correlated or logically interrelated in many ways — whereas concepts can only either include or exclude one another. There seems a tendency to think of Kelly as an illiberal person, who is trying to plead for a black-and-white world in which there are no shades of grey. In fact, Kelly insisted that constructs could be used in a *scalar mode*, while still being bipolar in origin. Thus, the famous 'shades of grey' stem from the construct *black* versus *white.* It is interesting to note that in terms of choice and decision, we invariably break back from scalar modes of construing (which are most useful when we are speculating about and investigating a problem) to bipolar modes of construing. We may spend a long time, if we have to get the piano through the door, in measuring, in most exquisite scalar mode, all kinds of dimensions, but eventually we have to decide that the bloody thing will either *go through* or it will *not go through*.

When we come to examine Kelly's invention of grid method as a way of exploring personal construct systems we will see that much is gained because we are able, mathematically, to represent a personal construct system by viewing it as made up of *bipolar* constructs.

Choice corollary: *Persons choose for themselves that alternative in a dichotomised construct through which they anticipate the greater possibility for the elaboration of their system*.

This is the corollary whereby Kelly tucks the tail of his theoretical snake into its mouth. He thereby creates either a tautology or a complete and integrated theory.

If people are in business to anticipate events and if they do this by developing personal construct systems then they will move in those directions which seem to them to make most sense, that is directions which seem to *elaborate* their construct systems. Kelly pointed out that this elaboration may take the form of definition (confirming in ever greater detail aspects of experience which have already been fairly actively construed) or extension (reaching out to increase the range of the construct system by exploring new areas that are only very partially understood). It must be stressed that elaboration is sought in terms of the system as it exists at the time and that the corollary does not imply that we always elaborate successfully. We can over-define to a point where we suffer the death of ultimate boredom, circling in a ritual manner around the same area, or we can over-extend the system and suffer death by ultimate chaos.

It has been argued (Holland, 1970) that this corollary is untestable and therefore unscientific. It can be counter-argued that the corollary is testable if we know enough about the structure of a particular individual's system to predict his or her choices in terms of that system. However, it is true that the corollary only tells us that a person will *try* to move away from confusion and towards understanding. It does not tell us whether and why this should sometimes be in terms of extension and at other times in terms of definition. The corollary itself seems in need of definition, if not extension.

Range corollary: *A construct is convenient for the anticipation of a finite range of events only*.

This follows from the original assertion that constructs are bipolar and finite in number. Kelly is here stressing that he is not simply refurbishing the old notion of a concept. The *concept* of 'furniture' as a general abstraction includes tables, chairs, desks, commodes and so forth and contrasts with *everything* that is not included in the category of furniture. The *construct* of 'furniture' as used in a *particular context* would include tables, chairs and so forth *as contrasted with* say office equipment, or *as contrasted with* Georgian tables which are to be regarded as antiques. The whole construct would then *exclude* sunsets, battleships, acts of heroism and candyfloss which are *outside the range of convenience* of the construct; they are not subsumed under either pole of it.

Kelly used the term *focus of convenience* to indicate those things for which a construct was specifically developed. Thus, the construct 'honesty', for some people has, as its *focus of convenience*, keeping your fingers off other people's property and money. The *range of convenience* is all those things to which people might eventually find the construct applicable. Thus for some people 'honesty' may eventually be used in relation to political honesty, sexual honesty, aesthetic honesty and so forth. In later sections dealing with grid method, it will be seen how the range corollary, along with the dichotomy corollary and others, guides the construction of the instrument, which in its turn, provides operational definitions for some of the constructs of the theory.

Experience corollary: *A person's construction system varies as they successively construe the replication of events.*

Personal construct theory implies that people continually develop. Development is not simply the prerogative of children and adolescents as the tradition of 'developmental psychology' would have us believe. The experience corollary is obviously related to the choice corollary. A personal construct system is not a collection of treasured and guarded hallucinations, it is the person's guide to living. It is the repository of what people have learned, a statement of their intents, the values whereby they live and the banner under which they fight. A personal construct system is a theory being put to perpetual test. Thus many people may construe *secretive* versus *open* as aligned with *safe* versus *dangerous* and live within these terms until other aspects of reality (also as interpreted by their construct systems) force them to risk the dangers of being *open*. If they do not then experience the anticipated *dangers*, the link between these constructions may be weakened and that aspect of the system begin to modify. Systems flow and modulate continuously as do the theories of scientists. But, as will be shown in relation to constructs such as 'hostility', change is neither automatic nor conventionally logical.

We change our construct systems in relation to the accuracy of our anticipations. Predictions are sometimes proved correct, sometimes found wanting, sometimes turn out to be totally irrelevant in terms of the unfolding events. If we expect to be *loved* and find that we are *hated*, those constructions about ourselves which led us to anticipate being loved become suspect. Equally, if we expect to be *loved* and find that we are merely *treated courteously* then it may be that our whole use of the construction *loved-hated* was inappropriate and its *range of convenience* is in question. It should be noted that this is not necessarily a cold-blooded or articulate business. In changing our construction systems we are changing ourselves and we may experience the change as more a painful chaos than a logical exercise.

Kelly disputed the insistence that his theorising be seen as about 'thinking' or about 'purely rational man'. He considered the idea of re-writing construct theory so that its basic contentions would be the same, but the language style would be changed so that it became *A Theory of the Human Passions* (his proposed title for the book). The aim of such a book would have been to stress that he did not accept the construct of *thinking* versus *feeling* (see Bannister, 1977). As Kelly put it:

> The reader may have noted that in talking about experience I have been careful not to use either of the terms, 'emotional' or 'affective'. I have been equally careful not to invoke the notion of 'cognition'. The classic distinction which separates these two constructs has, in the manner of most classic distinctions that once were useful, become a barrier to sensitive, psychological inquiry. (Kelly, 1969a, p. 140)

Kelly's argument that construct systems change rapidly or slowly in relation to experience makes his psychology essentially a dynamic theory.

Modulation corollary: *The variation in a person's construction system is limited by the permeability of the constructs within whose range of convenience the variants lie.*

Kelly's psychology is a psychology of change. He argues that a person is a 'form of motion', not a static object which is occasionally kicked into movement. However, he is at pains to suggest parameters for change, and the modulation corollary is such a parameter. The construct *permeable-impermeable* refers to the degree to which a construct can assimilate new elements within its range of convenience and generate new implications. Some constructs, are, for most of us, fairly impermeable — we happily apply *fluorescent* versus *incandescent* to sources of light, but rarely find its range of convenience extendable. On the other hand, for most of us, a construct such as *good* versus *bad* is almost continually extending its range of convenience.

When we are faced by a 'new' situation, if we generally traffick in permeable constructs, we can use them to make sense out of the new events which confront us. If our constructs tend to be impermeable, we may take pains to make sure that we do not encounter 'new' situations or else we may force them into the existing system however bad the fit. Both permeable and impermeable constructs are useful in given contexts, but the corollary stresses that one of the dangers of being too precise is that it nails us to a particular precision.

Fragmentation corollary: *A person may successively employ a variety of construction subsystems which are inferentially incompatible with each other.*

Kelly is here suggesting a further parameter of change — a parameter that suggests that change is not and need not be 'logical' in the simple sense of that term. A construct system is a hierarchy and also a series of subsystems having varying ranges of convenience. Therefore, conclusions about the 'same' series of events can be drawn at levels which are not directly consistent with each other. This is elaborated by Bannister and Mair in the following terms:

Although the presence of permeable constructs may allow the variation of aspects of a person's construct system to accommodate new evidence, this does not mean that a person's system will be completely logically related, with every construct being implied by every other one. The way a person will behave today cannot necessarily be inferred from the way he behaved yesterday. A parent may kiss and hug a child at one moment, smack him a little later and shortly afterwards ignore him when he insists on showing off by excessive chattering. To the casual

observer, it may seem that one response could not be anticipated from the previous one and that grossly inconsistent
behaviour and constructions were being adopted by the parent.
This may be the case, but need not be so. Just because different
constructions do not seem consistent with each other and one
cannot be inferred from the other directly, it does not mean that
no consistency exists for the person involved or for some other
observer of the scene. When, for example, the parent's *super-
odinate* constructs concerning love and training are considered,
some thread of consistency in the various actions may be noted.
(Bannister and Mair, 1968, p. 22)

Folklore phrases such as 'you have to be cruel to be kind' seem to
recognise that inferential incompatibility at a subordinate level has
been resolved at a superordinate level, while 'you are trying to
have your cake and eat it' seems to designate a superordinately
unresolved incompatibility.

Commonality corollary: *To the extent that one person employs a
construction of experience which is similar to that employed by
another, their processes are psychologically similar to those of the
other person.*

This is the complement of the individuality corollary and stresses
that people are not similar because they have experienced similar
events; nor, for that matter, similar because they appear, along
some limited time line, to be manifesting similar behaviour; nor, yet
again, similar because they utter the same verbal labels. People are
similar because they construe — i.e. discriminate, interpret, see
the implications of events — in similar ways. They are similar with
respect to events which have the same meaning for them.

This is an interesting corollary in its implications for experimental psychology, since it implies that we do not need to put
people into the 'same' experimental situation in order to find out
whether they are similar or different. People in the 'same' situation may be behaving similarly for the time being, but attaching a
very different significance to their own behaviour and to the events
they are encountering. Our long-term predictions of identity, on
the basis of this temporary behavioural similarity, are likely to be
very much astray. On the other hand, to the degree that we can
explore and evaluate the personal construct systems of two people,
we may be able to determine similarities between them, having
observed them in apparently different situations.

Sociality corollary: *To the extent that one person construes the construction processes of another, they may play a role in a social process involving the other person.*

This is a key corollary in that it insists that interpersonal interaction is in terms of each person's understanding of the other. This is quite different from assuming that people can only interact when they have similar construction systems or are, in some sense, similar people. You may interact for a long time with a child and be very much playing a role in a social process with that child. This does not imply that our construct system is the same as the child's, only that your construct system gives you a meaningful picture of the child's construct system. Nor does it make a role a purely social construct, that is, see it as the acting out of a dialogue written for the two persons by the society in which they have been brought up. It sees each of us as attempting, in relation to other people, to be psychologists, whether we be good, bad or indifferent psychologists. In terms of our ideas about people's construct systems we may seek to inspire them, confuse them, amuse them, change them, win their affection, help them to pass the time of day or defeat them. But in all these and many other ways we are playing a role in a social process with them. Conversely, if we cannot understand other people, that is we cannot construe their construction, then we may *do* things to them but we cannot *relate* to them.

Types of Construct

The fundamental postulate and its corollaries formally define the theory of personal constructs. In addition, Kelly provided a systematic language for describing construing processes. He classified constructs according to the nature of their control over their elements, into *pre-emptive, constellatory* and *propositional*.

A pre-emptive construct is one which pre-empts its elements for membership in its own realm exclusively. Thus, pre-emptively, if this person is a homosexual he or she is *nothing but* a homosexual. This is a gross restricting of the elaborative possibilities of construing. Whether we meet it in psychotherapy, politics or embedded in our own way of viewing some aspect of our environment, it is essentially a denial of the right of other people and ourselves to re-view, re-interpret and see in a fresh light some part of the world around us.

A *constellatory* construct is one which fixes the other realm membership of its elements. This is essentially sterotyped or typological thinking and says that if this man is a *homosexual* then he must be *effeminate, artistic, degenerate* and a *menace to society*. Again, it reduces our chances of elaborating or reviewing our outlook — it is a kind of intellectual package deal.

Finally, Kelly talked of *propositional* constructs. These are constructs which carry no implications regarding the other realm membership of their elements. They are 'as if' constructs where we are prepared to recognise that we can look upon person X *as a homosexual* man and thereby make sense out of what he says and does. But we are recognising that this is only *one* way of viewing him and is not some final, absolute or all-comprehending truth. We can equally regard him *as a friend* or *as a confused man* or *as a chartered accountant*. When we use constructs propositionally our world becomes potentially richer and we are less likely to be trapped into conflict by the rigidity of our stance. Propositionality stresses the idea that constructs are essentially *hypotheses* (as argued by Tschudi, 1983) and not *rules* as suggested by Mischel (1964).

Be it noted that this section has been written in a somewhat 'pre-emptive' manner in that reference is repeatedly made to constructs as *being* this or that, when clearly what is being talked about is the capacity of persons to use their constructs in a pre-emptive, propositional or constellatory *mode*.

General Diagnostic Constructs

Personal construct psychology is concerned with constructions about constructions. It makes psychology a meta-science, a way of making sense out of the ways in which people make sense of their world. Thus, it carries a number of constructs about construing and these include *dilation* versus *constriction*. This dimension sees persons as either broadening their view of the world in order to reorganise it on a more comprehensive level or constricting their view in order to minimise apparent incompatibilities.

It is important to understand that such dimensions as this do not have 'healthy' and 'unhealthy' ends. They are not to be confused with the constructs of the logician who is busily sorting out 'good' from 'bad' thinking. A person can dilate successfully and become a larger personality or extend out into chaos. A person may constrict and thereby make more controllable their world or move towards an increasingly impoverished world.

Another important construct of this type is *tight* versus *loose* construing. Kelly defines a tight construct of one which leads to unvarying predictions, whereas a loose construct is one which leads to varying predictions but which nevertheless can be identified as a continuing interpretation. Most technical discriminations are tight constructs, for example, *electrical* versus *diesel*, whereas many evaluative constructs appear loose, for example, *beautiful* versus *ugly*. The power output of a diesel engine can be accurately predicted, whereas the fate of a person as beautiful or ugly may be anybody's guess.

Tightening and loosening is a process whereby we can elaborate our construct systems and deal with the kaleidoscope of events that confront us; it is not any kind of choice between a right and a wrong way of doing things. The failure of psychologists to develop their own discipline by alternating between tight and loose construing is discussed in the following terms:

It is one of the most marked and disastrous characteristics of current psychology that there has been a cleavage into loose and tight *types of psychology*. This is to say that many psychologists fail to move repeatedly through the cycle but rather take up a permanent intellectual residence at one or other end of the cycle.

Thus, we have almost totally loose circumspective psychologies such as Freudian or Existential psychology. This is the kind of speculative, vague psychologizing which leads to papers of the *Unconscious aggression and overt sexual fantasies as quasi-religious substrata for international conflicts* type. At the other end of the spectrum we have the tight world of the pure learning theorist dealing in the highly defined and fragmentary and providing us with the *Short term memory for T mazes under electrically induced stress conditions in the decorticate woodlouse* type of paper. Thus, psychologists tend to take up residence and spend their lives with either the vaguely significant or the specifically irrelevant. They do not recognize that it is a continuous movement between loose and tight construing that enables the arguments which constitute a science to elaborate. This kind of frozen positioning seems to underlie much of the tough minded *versus* tender minded argument in science and is obviously referred to by phrases concerning the problem of vitality of material *versus* precision of method. (Bannister, 1970, p. 59)

Emotion As Actual or Impending Change

A common charge levelled against personal construct theory, even by those who admire it (e.g. Bruner, 1956), is that it is too 'mentalistic'. It is argued that Kelly's description of construct systems is purely a description of 'thinking' and thereby deals with only one aspect of the person, the 'rational' aspect. But Kelly did not accept the cognition-emotion division as intrinsically valid. It is a jargon descendant of the ancient dualities of *reason* versus *passion, mind* versus *body, thinking* versus *feeling* which has led to dualist psychologies. Personal construct psychology is an attempt to talk about people in a unitary language. We must not misunderstand the theory and assume that constructs are simply words, because the theory itself is systematic, articulate and rational. We may find that we can do much more without the cognition-emotion distinction than we have been able to do with it.

Kelly seeks to deal with the kind of problems which are, in both common-sense psychology and most modern psychology, dealt with in terms of the concepts of 'emotion' or 'drive' or 'motivation', but he remains within the general framework of his own theory and does not have recourse to extraneous concepts. 'Emotion' is a hydraulic concept, a vision of some kind of ginger pop fizzing about the human system and it sets up a kind of dichotomy in psychological theory which makes for very great problems. So a construct is not a 'thought' or a 'feeling'; it is a discrimination. It is part of the way you stand towards your world as a complete person. 'Emotion' is our experience of, or resistance to, change.

In order to avoid this dualism Kelly focuses our attention on certain specific constructs, namely *anxiety, hostility, guilt, threat, fear* and *aggressiveness*, but defines them all as aspects of construct systems in a state of change. His specific definitions are as follows.

Anxiety

Anxiety is awareness that the events with which one is confronted lie mostly outside the range of convenience of one's construct system.

We become anxious when we can only partially construe the events which we encounter and too many of their implications are obscure. Sex for the chaste, adulthood for the adolescent, books for the illiterate, power for the humble and death for nearly all of us, tend to provoke anxiety. It is the *unknown* aspects of those things that go bump in the night that give them their potency. This definition is reasonably specific, but it does not involve us in thinking of anxiety as some sort of separate factor inside us. The 'separate factor' theory is implied in common-sense statements such as 'He was driven by his anxiety' or psychological statements which talk about a person's 'level of anxiety' as if it were a permanent trait at a given degree of intensity. Moreover, Kelly's is a purely psychological definition of anxiety which does not require us to mix our metaphors further by recourse to physiological constructs.

Hostility

Hostility is the continued effort to extort validational evidence in favour of a type of social prediction which has already been recognised as a failure.

There are times when, if our construct system is to be preserved intact, we simply cannot afford to be wrong. If we acknowledge that some of our expectations are ill-founded, we might have to modify or abandon the constructions on which these expectations were based. But if these constructions are central to the whole of our stystem, we might well be faced with chaos if we abandon them, as we have no alternative way of viewing our situation. In such a position we are likely to become *hostile*, to extort evidence, to bully people into behaving in ways which confirm our predictions. We cook the books and refuse to recognise the ultimate significance of what is happening.

Hostility may appear in many forms. We may mistreat our neighbour's so that they counter-attack and provide 'proof' of the cherished theory that they are enemies. We may simply deny the validity of *the source* of evidence which is too crucially disconfirming. It can take the form of the overt paranoid delusion which uses a 'conspiracy' theory so that all evidence is controvertible. We cease to be hostile only when we can find alternative ways of interpreting ourselves and our situation. That is to say, only when we find some way of making sense and so avoid plunging into chaos.

Hostility is thus defined in terms of its self-preserving function for the individual who is hostile, rather than as a largely inexplicable, antagonistic emotion.

Guilt

Guilt is the awareness of dislodgement of the self from one's core role structure.

The term 'core role structure' refers to that system of constructs which deals specifically with the self. Core role constructs are those by which we evaluate the central aspects of our own behaviour; the personal issues with which we are most concerned; the ways in which we try to anticipate our own future directions and activities. Thus, if we find ourselves doing, in important respects, those things we would not have expected to do if we were the kind of person we always thought we were, then we suffer from guilt.

Note that the level of abstraction of this definition of guilt is high enough to free us from any need to refer to particular moral codes or cultural standards. We may feel guilty because we find ourselves doing those things which *other* individuals or social reference groups might well consider 'good' things to do. To live in a world where we cannot understand and predict others can be terrifying. How much more terrifying is it to find that we cannot understand and predict ourselves. It is, therefore, not surprising that the awareness that we are about to become a mystery to ourselves may produce the kind of ritualistic and rule-ridden behaviour (hostile behaviour in Kelly's sense of the term) which is typical of those who are experiencing guilt.

Threat

Threat is the awareness of an imminent comprehensive change in one's core structures.

Just as we have a particular core group of constructs by which we try to understand ourselves (core role structures), so we have constructs which subsume the most important aspects of the external world for us and which, when invalidated, produce a feeling of threat. We are threatened when our major beliefs about the nature of our personal, social and practical situation are invalidated and the world around us appears about to become chaotic.

Threat is an extremely important construct for anyone engaged in attempts to help other people. For example, the psychotherapist in an enthusiasm to change what is considered to be the restrictive and poorly developed ideas of the client, may plunge the client into over-hasty experimentation and thereby overly threaten him. The client may then either become hostile and resist all change or may plunge into the kind of chaos that earns him the title of psychotic. By threatening, in the personal construct sense of the term, we do psychological violence to a person.

Fear

Fear is the awareness of an imminent incidental change in one's core structures.

When only a more peripheral part of our world becomes meaningless and unpredictable, we experience fear. Our super-ordinate constructions are not invalidated, so we have no sense of being overwhelmed; but an area of darkness opens up before us and however circumscribed it may be, we feel fear at the impending change.

Aggressiveness

Aggressiveness is the active elaboration of one's perceptual field.

It is interesting to note that Kelly is here attempting to define aggression (and similarly attempts to define hostility) in terms of what is going on *within the individual* rather than in terms of other people's reactions to the individual. Thus, we are being aggressive when we actively experiment to check the validity of our construing; when we extend the range of our construing (and thereby our activities) in new directions; when we are exploring. Obviously from the point of view of the people around and about us, this can be a very uncomfortable process and they may well see it as an attack upon them and handle it as such. But in tems of the aggressive person's construction system, it is essentially an extending and elaborating process and therby the *opposite* of hostility.

The Construct of Emotion

Just as there is no onus on Kelly (or any other theorist) to build a general concept of 'emotion' into his theory, he or she is not obliged to provide exact equivalents for particular 'emotions'. However, a theory can be required to provide explanations for the kinds of problem-phenomena which are dealt with elsewhere under the rubric of this or that 'emotion'. Consider, for example, the kind of commitment which, in lay psychological theories, is dealt with under the concept of 'being in love'. From a personal construct viewpoint we might look on love as a form of role relationship. This does not mean that the two people concerned are simply acting out socially prescribed parts but that they are aggressively elaborating themselves — their core role structures — by experimenting with their understanding of each other.

'Being in love' is probably the situation in which most of us experience the greatest possibility of really elaborating ourselves and thereby take our greatest personal risk. In living out the relationship we put to the test our implicit interpretation of the nature of the other. We thereby extend our understanding of ourselves since we use another's reaction to us (filtered through our interpretation of them) in developing a picture of ourselves. However, since core role constructs are central to 'being in love', much is at risk. If our core construing is validated, we may elaborate and become truly a larger person — if we are invalidated, we may need to become hostile in order to avert chaos. We may then break up the relationship in order to deny the authenticity of the other person as a source of evidence. Alternatively a love affair could be developed on a hostile basis, in that the partners might bully each other into providing supporting evidence for a crumbling theory of themselves. Then no genuine risk is taken, no hypothesis is ventured; the evidence is worthless because the witnesses have bribed each other.

A commentary on love in these terms may seem inappropriate because it is 'rational' and love is said to be 'irrational', but such a view confuses event with interpretation. Kelly argues:

The man in love may see nothing rational in his experience, and he may go so far as to regard himself as the unwitting victim of psychodynamics or love potions. But that does not mean that we must limit ourselves to the same terms he uses. Our job is to understand his experience in general, not merely to simulate it in particular. To do this with any perspicacity we must devise our own constructions. Our constructs must enable us to subsume his constructs, not merely simulate them. If he thinks in terms of psychodynamics, that is something we ought to understand and appreciate. But it is not necessary for us to resort to psychodynamic explanations ourselves in order to understand his construct of 'psychodynamics'. (Kelly, 1977, pp. 2-3)

Stressing the redefinition of emotion in terms which have to do with transition, process and change, Kelly developed the idea of the circumspection-pre-emption-control cycle (CPC cycle). Kelly thus emphasises the way in which construct systems move and flow. Initially we circumspect the field (dream, imagine, speculate) in order to select out (pre-empt) certain issues as crucial and decide what kind of situation we are in. Finally we move to control, the point at which we make active choices which are to be elaborated. We decide not only what construct will cover the situation, but which pole of that construct will give us the best anticipatory base for action.

These constructs about transition all seem, in some measure, to relate to the traditional definitions of anxiety, guilt and so forth. But they are defined so as to be part of a unitary theory and so avoid the dualistic notion that inside each of us there are two persons, a 'reasoning' person and a 'feeling' person, these being unrelated except that each hinders and obstructs the progress of the other. For Kelly, such a dualism is a badly articulated attempt to cope with the fact that a person is a process and that at different stages in the process very different modes of experience and activity obtain (McCoy, 1977).

A Psychology of Personal Constructs

George Kelly entitled his major work *The Psychology of Personal Constructs* and thereby announced his intention of trying to create a new *psychology* rather than present a theory within the framework of orthodox psychology. The traditional tactic for containing revolutionaries is to 'put them in their place' so, not surprisingly, the standard textbook authors have sought to diminish Kelly's claim and have listed his work as one more 'cognitive' theory. Such a categorisation is in line with the tradition in psychology which argues that you cannot talk about the whole person and must first divide up the person into cognition, motivation, perception, memory, emotion and so forth, and all psychologists must then decide to which segment they want to stake a claim.

In this book the terms and formal aspects of construct theory are given in full as an appendix but it is essential in evaluating them to bear in mind what is meant by a 'construct'. A construct is not a verbal label. Constructs can be pre-verbal (developed before the child had a labelling system at all), they can have partial verbal labels as when one pole is named but there is no verbal tag whereby one can recognise the opposite pole. A person may have verbal labels for constructs at one level but be unaware of the lines of relationship and implications between different parts of their construct network. This constitutes our 'unconscious', endowing us with both resources and problems that we cannot readily put into words. A construct is essentially a discrimination which a person can make. Personal construct psychology is an attempt to understand the way in which each of us experiences the world, to understand our 'behaviour' in terms of what it is designed to signify and to explore how we negotiate our realities with others.

Kelly defines construing as a person's attempt to transcend the obvious:

> To transcend the obvious — this is the basic psychological problem of man. Inevitably it is a problem we must all seek to solve, whether we fancy ourselves as psychologists or not. What has already happened in our experience may seem obvious enough, now that we have been through it. But literally it is something that will never happen again. It can't, for time refuses to run around in circles. If then, as we live our lives, we do no more than erect a row of historical markers on the spots where we have had our experiences, we shall soon find ourselves surrounded by a cemetery of monuments, and overburdened with biographical mementoes.
>
> But to represent an event by means of a construct is to go beyond what is known. It is to see that event in a way that could possibly happen again. Thus, being human and capable of construing, we can do more than point realistically to what has happened in the past; we can actually set the stage for what may happen in the future — something, perhaps in some respects, very different. Thus we transcend the obvious! By construing we reach beyond anything that man has heretofore known — often reach in vain, to be sure, but sometimes with re-markable prescience. (Kelly, 1977, p. 4)

Psychology and Values

A theoretical framework in psychology inevitably proposes values. Incantatory insistence on being purely 'objective' does not enable us to escape the moral issues which are implicit in psychology. The declared aims of science — prediction and control — have moral connotations immediately we realise that it is human beings that psychologists are proposing to predict and control.

A psychological theory is inevitably not only a statement about people, it is an attitude towards them, a way of relating to them. The view of you as a mechanism, implicit in learning theory, can naturally be extended to support a manipulative attitude towards you and society. The Freudian portrait of you as essentially infantile, trapped in your inadequate attempts to deal with your sexual, aggressive, destructive and death-seeking drives is also an evaluation of you. It places the psychoanalysed psychoanalyst in the position of priest to penitent where other people are concerned. Personal construct psychology can be seen as valuing people and proposing a relationship between so-called psychologist and so-called subject — a relationship which is aimed at challenging and liberating people rather than diminishing them.

It is true that construct theory is an optimistic theory in that it envisages the optimal as well as the minimal person and in that it proposes itself as an elaborative tool which we might use to extend our own possibilities. However, it enables us to offer explanations for people at their most vicious as well as at their most inspiring. People do truly follow their constructions to the point where, if they construe others as being something substantially less than human, they are thereby enabled to torment and destroy them. Thus, the family-loving concentration camp guard is able to go cheerfully about his diabolical business.

In the following chapters examples will be given of how aspects of this psychology have been or might be used in an effort to understand the person. Wherever there is repetition this is not for its own sake, but rather it underlines the contention of this psychology that a person is a totality and cannot readily be segmented into category headings.

Obviously the ultimate value and fate of the theory will be decided by how useful people find it as experimental psychologists, as therapists, as individuals, but it is clear that its visible scope and implications merit exploration.

2 THE PERSON IN PSYCHOLOGY

> Speech is not what one should desire to understand. One should
> know the speaker . . . The deed is not what one should desire
> to understand. One should know the doer . . . Mind is not what
> one should desire to understand. One should know the thinker.
> (Kanshitaki, *Upanishad*, iii, 8)

Personal construct psychology takes the person to be the
irreducible unit. The fundamental postulate reads: 'A *person's*
processes are psychologically channelised by the ways in which
they anticipate events' [our italics]. Kelly continues:

> This term [person] is used to indicate the substance with which
> we are primarily concerned. Our first consideration is the indi-
> vidual person rather than any part of the person, any group of
> persons, or any particular processes manifested in the person's
> behavior. (Kelly, 1955, p. 47)

It is significant that ten out of the eleven elaborate corollaries
make specific reference to the 'person'.

Traditional psychology is not, in the main, about persons. By
making the person the central subject-matter of psychology, construct theory changes the boundaries and the content of the existing science. However, before we consider what psychology has
been about (while it was not being about persons), let us attempt a
brief description of *the person*. Let us begin, not by looking at
other people to see whether we are going to allow them the dignity
of being persons, but by deriving an initial definition from looking
at ourselves.

It is argued that *you* consider *yourself* to be a person in that:

1. You are convinced of your own separateness from others, you
rely on the privacy of your own consciousness.

2. You are convinced of the integrity and completeness of your experience in that you believe that all parts of it are ultimately relatable because you are the experiencer.

3. You are convinced of your own continuity over time, you believe that in a significant sense you are the *same* person as you were when you were a child, you possess your own biography and live in relation to it.

4. You are convinced that your actions are causal, that you have purposes, that you intend and thereby you accept a partial responsibility for the effects of what you do.

5. You are convinced of the separate existence of other persons by analogy with yourself, you assume a comparability of subjective experience between yourself and others.

The Focus of Traditional Psychology

Whether or not psychologists harbour the convictions we have listed above, many of them certainly choose to look on others not as persons but as moving objects, explicable in essentially mechanical terms. Personal construct theory argues that we will understand, explain and predict more about people, particularly over the course of time, if we centre our thinking on the idea of a 'person'. This is quite apart from the argument that it would be gracious so to do. Yet much of traditional psychology has achieved a rather inadequate and miserable statement of its subject because it has declined to use the idea of a person (Bannister, 1970). What then have psychologists studied instead of studying the person?

Behaviour

Psychologists have studied 'behaviour'.

The reverence with which 'behaviour' is spoken of in psychology probably stems from the half-expressed conviction that behaviour alone is 'real' and psychology itself is a mass of 'concepts'. Psychologists seem to fear that unless we cling steadfastly to behaviour, our whole discipline may turn out to be a ghastly, ghostly and, above all, unscientific misadventure.

The philosophical assumption of the psychology of personal constructs are explicit and they include an acceptance of a reality 'out there'. It is not a solipsistic theory but it does argue that we cannot apprehend reality directly. We can only construe and interpret it, usefully or uselessly, inventively or routinely, humorously or soberly. The same is true of the reality we call 'behaviour'. Immediately we label it, assess it, or even select it by pointing to it, we have placed a construction upon it. The instant we begin to talk of a twitching toe we are already deep into the meaning of the construct system which defines 'twitching' and defines 'toe'. If we see a man walking along the street we may say that he is 'going to the cinema' or 'manifesting motor movement' or 'dawdling' or 'showing adient rather than abient behaviour', but whatever we say of what he is doing we shall have construed. We shall not have made some miraculous interpretation-free contact with reality. The intention of some phenomenologists to make truly non-presuppositional statements is but a dream.

True, 'behavioural' terms are at a low level of abstraction, but they are still terms *at a level of abstraction*. Moreover, constructs such as stimulus, response, reward, punishment, drive, negative and positive reinforcement, are all constructs at an extremely high level of abstraction, certainly at as high a level of abstraction as constructs like 'mind'. They are about as near to behaviour as the construct Neanderthal is to the chipped flint to which it is applied.

It is true that, in so far as science requires operational definitions and common sense demands that we get down to brass tacks, any psychological theory will have to wrestle with, and predict in terms of, behaviour. But instead of trying to treat behaviour in its own right, personal construct theory argues that behaviour must be related to the person who behaves. What people do, they do to some purpose and they not only behave but intend to indicate something by their behaviour.

Behaviour is seen not as a reaction but as a proposition, not as the answer but as the question. As Kelly (1970a) has pointed out, behaviour is an experiment and in behaving we are asking a question of our world — a person's behaviour will make little ultimate sense to us unless we understand the questions which they are asking. Behaviour, like words (referred to by psychologists as verbal behaviour), has *meaning* and changing, elaborating and negotiated meaning at that.

Comparative psychology

Psychologists have avoided studying us as persons by studying 'us the animal'. True, we *can* study 'us the animal' just as we *can* study 'us the organic system' as in physiology. Psychology as a 'biological science' presents us as one of the 'higher' animals. From this point of view it makes sense to study the rat, the cat, the pigeon, the octopus, the woodlouse and the cockroach because, in so far as we are seeing ourselves as an elaboration of these, what is discovered of them is at least potentially relevant.

But we are entitled to study human beings as anything we wish — it is our choice because sciences are invented not discovered. And if we wish to understand someone *as a person*, then comparative studies cannot have more than metaphorical relevance. From a personal construct point of view the upside-down anthropomorphism of comparative psychology is properly the domain of the biologist or zoologist. Such studies, however competent or thoughtful, are in a language which renders them largely irrelevant to the understanding of you as a person. They are *psychologically* as useful as Aesop's *Fables* (though far duller).

The futility of the attempt to erect psychological constructs on the basis of biological elements is exemplified by Vince's (1967) study entitled 'Respiration as a factor in communication between quail embryos'. The key point here is the curious use of the term 'communication'. The study showed that the 'clicking' of quail eggs increases in speed as hatching time approaches. Within the clutch of quail eggs, the faster clickers speed up the slower clickers and the slower clickers slow down the faster clickers, the result being that the quail eggs hatch out more or less together. From a utilitarian point of view — in avoiding the mother quail being faced simultaneously with wandering chicks and incubating eggs — this seems a reasonable arrangement. As a purely zoological study the research seems admirable.

However, why the term 'communication'? Avalanches of stones moving down a mountainside presumably work on something like the same basis, in that fast stones are slowed down by collision with slow stones and slow stones are speeded up by collision with fast stones, the net result being that the stones tend to arrive at the bottom of the mountain somewhat together. However, we do not talk about the stones 'communicating' and we would be likely to sniff at a paper called 'Collision as a factor in communication between avalanching stones'. The term 'communication' seems to have very little meaning when applied to the embyro quail beyond that which it would have for the avalanching stone. Certainly it can carry little of the meaning that we are entitled to give it in a psychological context.

To say that a rat learns is true; to say that a person learns is true. Given problematics like language and consciousness, to say that both 'learn' is a kind of pun.

Let us note that the argument here is not about whether we are animals or not. Certainly we are animals, just as we are a collection of chemicals, an organic system and a mass of whirling electrons. The argument is whether it would be more rewarding for all concerned if psychologists studied us 'as animals' or studied us 'as persons' (Bannister, 1981).

Social psychology

In so far as it has involved a study of interpersonal interaction and used concepts implying a high level of consciousness such as 'attitude', social psychology has contributed to our understanding of us as persons. Indeed, it may be that most of the ideas relevant to a study of the person are at present to be found under the rubric of social psychology. However, psychologists have followed custom in establishing social psychology as a mini-psychology in its own right and have thereby hindered the development of a general psychology of persons. Equally, in making the *group* their focus of convenience, social psychologists have lost much of the meaning of the individual person within the group and the meaning of the group to the individual person.

Consider for example what social psychologists have made of the potentially invaluable idea of 'role' by seeing it too completely in group terms. Kelly put it as follows:

Role can be understood in terms of what the person *himself* is doing rather than in terms of his circumstances. There are two traditional notions of role, one the very old notion that role is a course of action which is articulated with the actions of others, so that together you and the other person can produce something. The more recent notion proposed by sociologists and other theorists is that a role is a set of expectations held by others within which a man finds himself encompassed and surrounded. Personal construct theory tries to put role within the context of something a person himself is doing and it springs from a notion that one may attempt to understand others in terms of their outlooks just as a personal construct theory psychologist tries to understand human beings in terms of their outlooks.

So anyone who attempts to understand others in terms of the outlooks they have, rather than their behaviours only, may indeed play a role. This isn't to say that he tries to conform to their outlooks, he may even try to stand them on their heads, but if he tries to understand others by putting on their spectacles and then does something, then that which he does could be considered as a role. So we have three notions of role here. The oldest notion, the notion of a course of activity articulated with the action of others, I suppose that notion could be tied up with the notion of man as the economic entity, 'the economic man'. The more recent notion of man surrounded by a set of expectations, I suppose you can say would be a notion that would undergird the society which has seen itself composed of 'ideological man' conforming to ideas, ideologies. But if we follow the notion of role that comes out of construct theory, I wonder if we might not develop the notion of man as a society composed of 'empathic man' or 'inquiring man'. Men who seem to understand and do it by active inquiry, using their own behaviour not as something to act out, but as a means of understanding their world. (Kelly, 1966)

Kelly is here pointing to the sociality corollary which says that 'to the extent that one person construes the construction processes of another, they may play a role in a social process involving the other person'. This definition relates the 'individual' to the 'social' and makes role more than simply a socially prescribed dialogue. Indeed the integration of social with individual or general psychology (their original separation has impoverished both) might well centre on re-thinking, in personal construct terms, the idea of role, along with Kelly's propositions about sociality, individuality and commonality (see, for example, Karst and Groutt, 1977, Adams-Webber, 1979, Stringer and Bannister, 1979).

Personality

The study of personality would seem to be inescapably the study of the person and yet again, by demoting it to an area *within* psychology, the equivalence of the terms 'psychological' and 'personal' has been lost. If psychology were truly the study of the person, we would no longer have 'personality' as a separate topic, any more than we would have work on 'problem-solving' which did not include the solving of personal problems, or have 'person perception' as a special and rather suspect part of the general study of perception.

The castrating effect of separating personality off as a mini-psychology in its own right is perhaps best seen in the curiously named study of 'individual differences', which turns out to be the study of group samenesses. Here we have focused on the establishment of general dimensions, at some point along which all individuals can be placed, rather than on a study of the dimensions which each individual develops in order to organise their own world. Mair comments thus:

> Psychologists, of course, repeatedly involve people in their experiments, but relatively few experimenters seem concerned with them as individuals, preferring generally to see each one as part of a fairly anonymous subject pool. So widely accepted is this view that some may not think it very important that there are striking features of individual people as we know them from everyday experience to which 'experimental' or 'scientific' psychology pays little heed. My own belief, however, is that whatever else it may concern itself with, psychology should be concerned centrally with defining and elaborating individual experience and action. In suggesting that psychology should be fundamentally about individuals, I am not proposing an isolationist, anti-social view since I am convinced of the irretrievably interpersonal nature of each person's system for organizing and making sense of himself and the world around him. Neither am I suggesting that groups should be excluded from the study, but wish only to draw attention to the fact that more often than not the study of groups is merely the superficial study of a number of individuals at the same time; the presence of so many people being surreptitiously used as a justification for the impersonal and insensitively standardized appproach to any particular individual involved. (Mair, 1970, p. 245)

The attempt to encompass the person within the study of personality is additionally bedevilled by the persistence of trait psychology. The habit of seeing others in a rather simple, rigid and typological manner has stunted the life of many individuals and its formalisation in psychology has had a similar effect upon the discipline. When you say, in trait terms, 'Flora *is* bad-tempered', you are locking the bad temper into Flora so that you do not have to face the issue of the bad temper that is *between* you and Flora. Equally, when, as psychologists, we ask 'is this person's behaviour consistent?' (in trait personality language), we mean consistent *in our terms* not consistent *in her terms*.

The segmented person

Long ago many of the old and apparently discredited 'faculties' of faculty psychology won their final victory when they were transmuted and each attained the status of a mini-psychology in its own right. The standard chapter headings of memory, cognition, motivation, perception, emotion, the senses and so forth, are the ultimate denial of the person as the subject-matter of psychology. They substitute for the person functions, to be studied separately, in spite of the fact that they cannot be *lived* separately. Any experimental psychologist who has ever done a study of, say, memory, has watched his/her stubborn subjects continue to cognise, emote, perceive, sense and so on, even though the experiment called upon them only to remember.

Consider the particular study of 'memory' as an area. It largely began with the work of Ebbinghaus who sought scientific purity by using nonsense syllables as his material to be remembered. But *as a person* we do not choose to remember nonsense, though *as an experimental subject* we might. Nearly 50 years later Bartlett clearly argued that memory be placed back in the context of the person (note he uses 'we' in the final paragraph of his classic work):

> I have written a book preoccupied, 'in the main', with problems of remembering and its individual and social determination. But I have never regarded memory as a faculty, as a reaction narrowed and ringed round, containing all its peculiarities and all their explanations within itself. I have regarded it rather as one achievement in the line of the ceaseless struggle to master and enjoy a world full of variety and rapid change. Memory, and all the life of images and words which goes with it, is one with the age-old acquisition of the distance senses, and with that development of constructive imagination and constructive thought wherein at length we find the most complete release from the narrowness of present time and place. (Bartlett, 1932, p. 314)

It seems likely that the attraction of the segmented person and the chapter-heading approach to psychology lies in the freedom from the discipline of theory which such an approach offers. The intellectual carve-up encourages an empirical approach marked by cafeteria thinking. The psychologist arbitrarily defines the problem in convenient and empirical terms and selects, on a cafeteria basis, whatever concepts suit the immediate purpose. He or she then solves the problem in terms as arbitrary and *ad hoc* as those in which it was originally posed. This kind of procedure has some short-term applied pay-offs, but it grossly inhibits the growth of a science.

Physiological psychology

Physiological psychology represents a complete evasion of the person as an issue in psychology, since the person is no more their cerebral cortex than their left earhole (cf. Bannister, 1968).

Perhaps the fascination which neurophysiological concepts have for many psychologists stems from their yearning to have direct contact with and 'know' reality, rather than accept that it can only be construed. In some strange way, it seems to be thought that because the concepts of physiological psychology refer to tiny 'units beneath the skin', we have here the kind of 'reality' that physicists are assumed to have when they talk of atoms and molecules. Bannister argued:

> Perhaps the key to misconceptions in this type of reductionism is the notion that problems (or phenomena or areas of study) exist somehow independently of the sciences which define them. A chemical 'problem' is one which is stated *in chemical terms* and a psychological problem is so because it represents alternative lines of implication for a group of *psychological* concepts (this is why it is a problem). As such it cannot be solved in non-psychological terms. What may happen is that some other problem involving similar operational definitions is set up in other (e.g. neurophysiological) terms. This can be solved in such neurophysiological terms but the psychologically defined problem has not thereby been 'transcended' or 'reduced', it remains to be solved in its own terms (Bannister, 1970b, p. 415)

Thus, when psychologists study brain damage they attempt to mimic the physiologist who is sensibly committed to studying us *as organic systems*, not *as persons*. Psychologists study how damage to the brain causes defects which can be construed in semi-mechanical terms, for example, motor slowness, slurring of speech, visual difficulties and so on. At best they use a fractional-functional model as in studies of memory failure. It is significant that they do not often study what 'brain-damaged' people make of themselves *as people* living with these handicaps. (A notable exception is Gardner's book *The Shattered Mind*, 1977.) Do brain-damaged persons remake their ideals from those of Napoleon to those of St Francis? How do they see their limitations? These and related questions are validly *psychological*. The currently popular questions are properly the outer boundaries of neurophysiology.

The outlawed person

This discourse on the ways in which psychologists (intentionally or unintentionally) have excluded the person from their field of study still leaves us with the question of why they have done this.

Firstly, making the person the centre of study might well preclude us from playing 'the science game' as it is now understood. We would have to re-imagine our experiments instead of mimicking the procedures of the natural scientist in a concrete manner. This, because persons (as distinct from functions or behaviours or physiological readings or rats) are potentially as much ex-perimenters as we are. Thus, the traditional 'experimenter-subject' roles would have to be abandoned. We could, for example, review our picture of the behaviour therapist as he or she 'shapes' the mute schizophrenic's speech by making gifts of sweets or cigarettes contingent upon the production of speech. We might have to recognise the validity of the mute schizophrenic as a person who is 'shaping' the psychologist's behaviour by making the gift of speech contingent upon sweet- or cigarette-giving.

Secondly, so long as we continue to exclude the person from the discourse of psychology, we can continue to ignore the relationship between our professional and personal lives. Mair has pointed out:

> The dilemma facing psychologists who wish to acknowledge the specifically human features of those they study (rather than the features men share with animals) is a dilemma just because psychologists too are human. When they recognize that their subjects share many of the concerns and capacities of ex-perimenters, they must also appreciate that they, as ex-

perimenters, share the limitations of ordinary people. Psychologists, like other people, have to work within the bounds set by their own achievements and hope to extend their competence only through the means they are capable of employing. Each has a limited viewpoint, personal and often unacknowledged assumptions, preferred theories and explanations, favoured methods for raising and answering questions. Like others, a psychologist can only subsume the assumptions, theories, methods and actions of others in relation to his personal points of view and to the extent that his own sense-making system allows. (Mair, 1970a, p. 182)

Recognition that psychology is a science of persons invented by persons would involve us in making our personal values explicit in relation to professional issues. Currently personal values guide our professional lives — as inevitably they must — but are not avowed (Bannister, 1981).

Personal research

Salmon (1978) comments that much bad or dishonest psychological research or research undertaken as a ritualistic exercise, is born just because the researcher has no personal commitment to the area. The researcher concerned with morality in adolescence who misinforms his subjects and secretly observes them through one-way screens could not do this if the research question had meant anything to the researcher personally. Salmon argues further that the relationship between research students and their research would have a different meaning if personal values and involvements were made explicit. She wants to challenge

the longstanding tradition in psychology of detachment and neutrality in research, and, on the contrary, to reject for research studentships those applicants who have no personal involvement in their proposed research. If a student does not actually care one way or another about what he may find out in his research, quite apart from the doubt this may cast on his being likely to complete the work, it certainly suggests that he will not be able to bring to it any of the personally significant meanings which in the end will give it any message it may have. (Salmon, 1978, p. 38)

It is the exploration of these meanings which should form the first part of the research project. She argues further that research within a personal construct psychology framework would look very different from its present form. Research would be about 'the process whereby people come to make sense of things'; it would involve working *with* and not *on* subjects; the constructions of the researcher would be explicitly stated in any formulations and inquiries; and the results obtained

> will be seen as less important, in the end, than the whole progress of the research itself — which, after all, represents one version of the process it is investigating. The crucial question, about any research project, would then be how far, as a process, it illuminated our understanding of the whole human endeavour to make sense of our lives, and how fruitful it proved in suggesting new exploratory ventures. (Salmon, 1978, p. 43)

The Re-focusing of Psychology

Clearly, a re-focusing of psychology on to the person does not mean a simple rejection of all that has gone before. Much of it can be reinterpreted to throw light on our understanding of persons, although, since psychology is an invention and not a discovery, we are under no obligation to carry forward everything that has ever been done in its name. It would be to our advantage to leave much behind. Such a re-focusing of psychology onto the person would make the work of psychologists much more interrelatable, so that viewpoints, methods, theories and hypotheses would often be competitive and cumulative. In the past, the carving-up of the field into mini-psychologies has allowed a 'live and let live' policy. Each psychologist has been free to stake their own claim and produce work which had no implications, nice or nasty, for the endeavours of those in other territories. This disintegrated but comfortable mode of developing the discipline might come to an abrupt end.

This then is the central feature of personal construct psychology. It is not a theory *within* psychology as at present practised. It is a proposal that the focus and boundaries of the discipline be redefined and it thereby explicitly challenges the basis of traditional psychology (Neimeyer, 1985).

3 EXPLORING THE PERSON

> The first thing the intellect does with an object is to class it along with something else. But any object that is infinitely important to us and awakens our devotion feels to us also as if it must be *sui generis* and unique. Probably a crab would be filled with a sense of personal outrage if it could hear us class it without ado or apology as a crustacean, and thus dispose of it. 'I am no such thing,' it would say 'I am myself, myself alone.'
> (William James, *The Varieties of Religious Experience: A Study in Human Nature*. Gifford Lectures, 1901-2)

The way we look at things determines what we *do* about measuring or changing those things; be it the problem child at school, racial prejudice, disturbed behaviour in the individual, or that indefinable concept 'personality'. We have discussed how psychologists have segmented the person, working within categories they have evolved to divide us into manageable bits — we learn (learning), perceive (perception), think (cognition), we have drives (motivation), and so forth. The person as an entity has been hooked on to these categories as an afterthought as in 'person perception'; or has been equated with their 'reinforcement history'; or has been regarded as a source of error variance sometimes annoyingly encountered when one is trying to measure generalities scientifically.

Theory Versus Eclecticism

While there are coherent theoretical frameworks for the psychologist to employ, many choose to mix parts of unrelated theories to account for our behaviour. Harsh things have been written about such eclecticism. Boring (1950) speaks of 'sheer eclectic laziness', and in 1929 referred to the 'eclectically-minded,

41

middle-of-the-road nonentity'. Allport (1964), in his paper 'The fruits of eclecticism — bitter or sweet?', defines eclecticism as 'a system that seeks the solution of fundamental problems by selecting and uniting what it regards as true in the several specialized approaches to psychological science'. He points out the great difficulty, if not the impossibility, of the task eclectics set themselves. They must somehow integrate a great diversity of results from very different levels of discourse.

One of the great illusions in psychology is that 'facts' can be added together and that, come the day of Jubilo, they will be united under one theoretical framework. Only if one works within a single theory can an integrated sequence of hypotheses be derived and the experimental findings added systematically to our knowledge. Pure 'fact' gathering is, in any case, a myth. The very selection of 'this' or 'that' fact as relevant to our understanding implies assumptions which constitute the psychologist's hidden, unformulated and probably internally contradictory theory.

The One or The Many As The Basis of Study?

Kelly's emphasis on the study of the individual person highlights a trend in psychology that started gathering momentum half a century ago. Increasingly it was realised that it is not only possible but also in many instances desirable to study the data from one individual (idiography) as well as data from a number of individuals (nomothesis).

Like all change, there has been considerable controversy over the merits of each approach (see, for example, du Mas, 1955, and Marceil, 1977) and there has been a tendency to regard either camp as wholly good or wholly bad depending on one's own commitment. Allport enlivened the debate in 1937 by remarking that nomothetic methods

> seek only general laws and employ only those procedures admitted by the exact science. Psychology in the main has been striving to make of itself a completely nomothetic discipline. The idiographic sciences, such as history, biography and literature, on the other hand, endeavour to understand some particular event in nature or in society. A psychology of individuality would be essentially idiographic. (Allport, 1937, p. 22)

Allport was thus concerned with the unique qualities of the individual person and saw the nomothetic approach as ignoring these qualities. But as time went on, the idiographic approach became limited to a description of methodology, that is, single-case studies as opposed to the collection of group data.

It is, and indeed has been for many a year, the fashion to use nomothetic methods, but increasingly psychologists have expressed dissatisfaction with the results obtained and the generalisations made. Their disquiet rests upon demonstrations that only under very special circumstances do 'averaged' curves have the same form as any of the 'individual' curves from which they are derived.

Baloff and Becker (1967) point out that Tryon was making this point about rat research in 1934 when he said that

> the intensive study of the average behaviour of a species . . . generally leads the . . . psychologists to ignore the more interesting differences between individuals from whom the 'average individual' is abstracted. The 'average' individual is, in fact, a man-made fiction, and the behaviour of a species can be properly understood only by considering variations in behaviour of all (or a random sample) of the individuals who are classed in it. (Tyron, 1934, p. 409)

Personality

Of all the categories used in psychology to describe people, that called 'personality' must surely be the most unsatisfactory. The concept seems to include almost every idea about us as people that has ever been suggested. Since what we measure is specified by our concept of what personality is, it is not surprising that psychologists split into a multitude of factions where its measurement is concerned. In 1937 Allport listed 50 meanings for personality and it is anybody's guess how many there are now. Hall and Lindzey's statement in 1957 is as applicable today: ' . . . no substantive definitions of personality can be applied with any generality . . . we submit that personality is defined by the particular empirical concepts which are a part of the theory of personality employed by the observer'. You pays your money and you takes your pick.

Specifications for a theory of personality

Kelly never makes explicit his definition of the term 'personality', but he repeatedly implies that our personality is our way of construing and experimenting with our personal world. But what he does do is provide 'design specifications' for a theory of personality.

In the first place, the perspective should be broad and the theory should be about something, otherwise the theorist 'may spend his time building a fancy theory about nothing; his theory will have no focus of convenience' (1955, p. 23). The focus of convenience of personal construct psychology is the psychological reconstruction of life, epitomised in the psychotherapeutic encounter. All theories have a range of applicability beyond their specific focus. Freud's theory focused on the psychodynamics of the neurotic individual, but its range has been extended to include interpretation and practice in art, literature and religion. Some theories have very limited ranges of convenience. Hull's theory of learning, for instance, broke down when attempts were made to extend it to cover personality.

The range of convenience of Kelly's theory is still being tested. It would seem to be of potential use wherever the subject (person) imposes meaning on an event. It is inapplicable in the demonstration of the Yerkes-Dodson law or the Skaggs-Robinson hypothesis. In neither case does the subject's construing of what they are being asked to do play any part in the experiments.

In a sense, this whole book is concerned with the range of convenience of personal construct theory. Impressions of its current range of convenience can be seen in the work being carried out in fields other than the clinical one. There is the study in linguistics of Baker (1979) on ways in which a person approaches the task of spelling as part of literate activity; Gillard's approach to history (1982, 1984), Orley's (1976) anthropological study of the meaning different classes of spirits have for Ganda villagers; Earl's (1983) application of the theory to economics; Gordon's (1977) study of thinking in profoundly deaf young men with restricted language; Eden, Jones and Sims' (1979) discussions about 'thinking' in organisations; Boxer's (1981) use of computer-assisted feedback in increasing understanding between managers; Thomas and Harri-Augstein's (1983; 1985) work on the whole field of learning and the use of computers; Lemon's (1975) investigation of linguistic development in bilingual Tanzanian school-children; and there are the accounts of people's perceptions of seaside resorts (Riley and Palmer, 1976; Stringer, 1976).

The second specification is that a theory should be fertile in creating new ideas: 'It should lead to the formulation of hypotheses; it should provoke experiments; and it should inspire invention' (Kelly, 1955, p. 24). The variety of topics just mentioned in relation to range of convenience suggests that this specification, at least, is being met in personal construct psychology. More detailed evidence can be found in Adams-Webber (1979) which reviews work carried out since 1955.

But along with stimulating ideas, the hypotheses generated should be testable. Only if more hypotheses are supported by experimental results than are negated can a theory remain alive. Kelly is of the opinion that a good psychological theory does not have to contain its own operational definitions but it should be capable of generating hypotheses that 'lead to research with operationally defined variables'.

Even though a theory should be all these things, it will ultimately prove to be redundant, so giving way to a theory that is richer, better able to explain the existing observations and lead to more precise hypotheses — an alternative construction. In this way a body of scientific knowledge develops. In this sense Kelly built into his theory the seeds of its own destruction.

Intelligence

It was through the development of the intelligence test that psychologists became regarded as measurers or psycho-metricians. And, for this, Binet must shoulder the main blame or praise. Binet had no explicit theory about what 'intelligence' was; he was primarily responding to an expressed need of the French government of the time. He was required to provide a means of identifying those children in France who needed special attention at school to help bring them up to the level of their peers.

Since that time, psychologists have broadened the range of convenience of the construct 'intelligence'. For it is a construct; it is one dimension people have constructed which enables them to sort out the individuals with whom they come into contact. In-telligence is now measured in adults and even rats. Psychologists have also been highly industrious in trying to establish both theoretical and operational definitions. That the work of psychologists has social and political significance is clearly shown by the public concern expressed over the work of Jensen and others relating **IQ** measures to race (e.g. Jensen, 1972).

Just as Kelly argues that the construct of motivation is not a useful starting point for psychologists (and it did indeed get them very bogged down in the analysis of the sex, hunger and thirst drives of the rat), so he argues that the notion of **IQ** has failed to be of general use. This is not because it cannot be measured, nor because it fails to correlate with certain other behaviours, but because it does not help in increasing our understanding of what people can do about themselves and about each other. Intelligence is regarded as a trait; we have studied something static with allegedly immutable characteristics. We have said that one group of people is less intelligent than another; that one child is below average in intelligence in comparison with a sample of children of the same age and background.

Kelly felt strongly that this was harmful and says:

> The child who is nailed down to the **IQ** continuum has just that much less chance of changing his teacher's opinion about him. If he is 'low', his unorthodox constructive ventures will never be given a thoughtful hearing; if he is 'high' his stupidities will be indulged as the eccentricities of genius. In formulating the construct of the IQ we have become enmeshed in the same net that immobilizes many a patient; we may have been caught in the web of our own construct system. Having been so careful to pin all persons down to a continuum with respect to which they can never change. We may now be confronted with a product of our own handiwork — a world full of people whom we cannot conceive of as changing, whom we can do nothing about! Is not IQ a distressingly unfertile construct after all? Should we not, therefore, take better care when we create the design specifications for future diagnostic constructs? (Kelly, 1955, p. 454)

Instead of nailing people down at whatever stage of life they are at, we should be studying the *process* that is leading the person to conduct his behavioural experiments in ways that are different from his peers. Having found out some of these differences, we can then go on to see what we can do to help him or her change — or, more importantly, what they might do to help themselves bring about change.

Creativity

Much has been written about the relationship between creativity and intelligence. For instance, Hudson (1968) described convergent thinkers as being good at conventional intelligence tests; specialising in physical sciences; holding conventional attitudes; having mechanical or technical hobbies; and being emotionally inhibited. In contrast to these people there are the divergent thinkers who are best at tests that do not have single answers; who specialise in arts subjects; who hold unconventional attitudes; who have interests mainly centred on people; and who are emotionally uninhibited.

Hudson (1970) showed the weakness of this trait dimension by demonstrating that boys could reverse roles if *instructed* to do so.

Kelly also had something to say on creativity but approached it from a very different angle. Since movement and change are the very essence of the psychology of personal constructs, Kelly saw creativity as being a cyclic phenomenon. The cycle 'starts with loosened construction and terminates with tightened and validated construction' (1955, p. 528). When we construe tightly, all events coming within the range of convenience of a particular construct are assigned very definitely to one pole of that construct or the other — there are no shades of grey. When we construe loosely, we are flexible, perceive subtle possibilites, and tolerate ambiguities. Thus scientists, or persons-as-scientists, who always indulge in tight construing, may have a massive concrete output to their credit. But they will never be able to produce new ideas, since creative thinking can only result from loosening the connection between constructs and realigning them in an unusual way. On the other hand, those who think loosely all the time cannot be creative either, since they are unable to tighten up on their ideas to the point at which they come into clear focus and can be tested. It is by living through succeeding cycles of loosening and tightening that we develop ourselves and our understanding of the world around us.

Hudson's convergent-thinking boy scientist is one who specialises in the use of tight construing; he minimises the importance of letting his hair down. But this does not mean he is *unable* to loosen. It may only mean that people the boy considers important consistently validate his constructions when he adopts a tight posture. That it is some form of socially prescribed behaviour is further suggested by Hudson's finding that boys do not see *themselves* as belonging, exclusively, to either 'science' or 'arts' groups; they see themselves as having the good qualities of both. This same process of opting one's self out of the stereotype to which others see us as belonging has been demonstrated in many other contexts (see Bannister, 1965; Fransella and Adams, 1966; Fransella, 1968, 1972; Hoy, 1973).

Measuring Personal Construct Relationships

Ever since they started to think of themselves as scientists, measurement has been at the forefront of psychologists' minds. One of the overriding problems in the field of personality has concerned the question 'what to measure?'. But there is no such difficulty with personal construct theory; the unit is clearly stated — it is the 'construct'. No doubt drawing on his training in mathematics, Kelly designed a technique whereby the mathematical relationships between constructs could be obtained (*repertory grid technique*). He even went so far as to provide the future user of the technique with his own method of non-parametric factor analysis (see Kelly, 1955, pp. 277-91).

But Kelly did not think methods of quantification were all there should be in the psychologist's tool-bag. Constructs can be elicited from an individual in conversation, from essays, from poetry, from journal papers. As a method for encouraging the person to delve deeply into themselves, Kelly described the *self-characterisation*. He considered that quantitative and qualitative methods of measurement were equally valid as ways of inquiring into a person's view of the world. But each has different networks of implication and will be discussed separately.

Repertory grids

The organisation corollary of the theory states that, for each individual, constructs do not form a chaotic jumble but are related into an integrated system. If it were not for this assumption, repertory grid testing would not be possible. A grid is a way of getting individuals to tell you, in mathematical terms, the coherent picture they have of, say, teachers. The first task, if this were your aim, might be to ask a particular pupil to think of three teachers and tell you some important way in which she sees two as being alike and thereby different from the third teacher. The pupil may differentiate between them in terms of sex. With three more teachers, the construct discrimination could be in terms of *lively* versus *boring*; next *intelligent* versus *stupid*; another being *doddering* versus *young*; and yet another *bossy* versus *free-and-easy* and so on until different combinations of teachers can produce no more new constructs.

You may now take all the teachers which the pupil construed and ask the pupil to tell you where each teacher stands in relation to each construct. At the end of all this you have a matrix of numbers indicating the interaction between teachers and constructs. When this has been done you can apply Kelly's own statistical procedure for analysing the matrix or any of the others now available (see Fransella and Bannister, 1977).

In its original form the technique was called the Role Construct Repertory Test. Here, the subject is asked to name 20 or 30 people they know who fit different role titles, such as 'teacher you dislike' and 'person you admire'. These people may also include parent figures, siblings, spouses and so forth. Those who fit role titles or the teachers in the example above are called *elements*. Constructs are then elicited by taking three elements at a time. In the Role Construct Repertory Test, the procedure ends there, having provided some insight into the way the person construes their interpersonal environment.

Kelly then extended this procedure to develop the Repertory Test. Here the role titles are written along the top of the grid matrix and the elicited constructs down the side. The subject simply places a tick in the cell if the particular person in a column can be described by the emergent pole of the construct in the row (e.g. *lively* rather than *boring*).

Misleading correlations can be produced if the ticks and voids in the matrix have a lopsided distribution. If only one person in terms of one construct is considered an *unprincipled lecher* and one other person is considered in terms of another construct as *doddering*, there would be a near match between the two rows in the matrix and statistically one would have the picture that virtually all dodderers are unprincipled lechers. This may not be precisely what the subject meant. Kelly had been aware of this difficulty and had suggested ways in which lopsided rows could be eliminated. Bannister (1959), however, preferred to modify the technique by forcing the subjects to divide the elements equally between two poles of the construct. Some people found this method rather artificial and since then it has become more common to use grids in which the elements are either ranked or rated in terms of the constructs. Note that solving the statistical problems presented by lopsidedness should not lead us to ignore lopsidedness in construing, as it is clearly an important psychological phenomenon in its own right. For instance, when one pole of a construct is 'submerged'.

Implication grids

A major revision of the theory and technique has been proposed by Hinkle (1965). He argued that constructs are defined by their implications and designed the Implications Grid or Impgrid to quantify such relationships. This grid differs from other forms in that there are no elements to be construed. Each construct is paired with every other construct to see whether one implies the other. This yields two types of information. One can find out what it means to a person to be a politician and also what things would imply being a politician. That is, a politician may mean being *hard-working, ruthless, two-faced* and *verbally fluent*, but none of these things need necessarily imply that one is a politician.

A modification of the Impgrid has been described by Fransella (1969 and 1972). Here, each pole of a construct is treated separately so that the implications of each can be established. This has proved particularly useful in the context of psychotherapy where it is important to know not only what a person thinks about the characteristics they see themselves as having, but also what it would mean to be different. If you are asking a person to change from being a stutterer to a non-stutterer or from being obese to being a normal weight, it is vital to have an idea of what the change is likely to imply; what sort of psychological world you are asking them to enter (e.g. Fransella, 1982). A procedure very similar to this bi-polar Implications Grid has been adapted by Honess (1977; 1979) for use with children. Honess (1978) has also compared the Implications Grid with other forms in terms of, for instance, comparability of scores obtained.

Laddering

Hinkle also described a procedure called 'laddering'. This is a form of construct elicitation in which the person is able to indicate the hierarchical integration of their personal construct system. For each construct elicited, the person is asked which pole of that construct they would prefer to be described by. For example, if they say that they would prefer to be *verbally fluent* as opposed to a *muddled speaker*, they are asked why it is preferable, *for them*, to be verbally fluent. If they say that *verbally fluent* people *are able to get ideas across* whereas *muddled speakers* only *confuse people*, then *get their ideas across* versus *confuse people* is another construct, superordinate to the first. The person is again asked the question why this is preferable and replies that there is *less likely to be misunderstanding* if you *get your ideas across*; 'why is that important?' — because there is *less likely to be a breakdown in communication*; 'why is that important?' — because *the only way to prevent people annihilating each other is to understand one another*.

This 'why' technique can start with any type of construct, be it about kinds of soap, opera, television programme or works of art — the end product will be some superordinate construct to do with one's philosophy of life. Equally, the laddered conversation can be directed downwards to more subordinate constructs by asking initially 'what constitutes verbal fluency' or questions of this kind. Landfield (1971) has explored this aspect in his pyramid technique.

Characteristics of the grid

Although many forms of repertory grid are now in use and others in the process of development (for details, see Bannister and Mair, 1968; Fransella and Bannister, 1977; Beail, 1985; Thomas and Harri-Augstein, 1985), they all have certain general characteristics in common.

1. They are concerned with eliciting from a person the relationships between sets of constructs, either in terms of construing *elements* (as in the Repertory Test, rank-order or rated forms) or by directly comparing construct with construct (as in Hinkle's Impgrid or Resistance-to-Change Grid).
2. The primary aim is to reveal the construct patterning for a person and not to relate this patterning to some established normative data. There is no reason why normative data should not be collected for some specific purpose as in the Grid Test of Thought Disorder (Bannister and Fransella, 1966), but the construing system of an individual is the prime focus.

3. There is no fixed form or content. It is called repertory grid *technique* and not *test* advisedly and the selection of the form and content is related to each particular problem. A grid designed to investigate how nomadic bushmen interpret their desert home would be pretty useless to suburban commuters, even in trans-lation, except perhaps to show that the commuters might have problems finding their way to work in the desert.

4. All forms are designed so that statistical tests of significance can be applied to the set of comparisons each individual has made. A basic assumption underlying the method is that the *psychological* relationships between any two constructs for a given person are reflected in the statistical association between them when they are used as judgemental categories.

Grid applications

Many uses of the grid will be discussed later in connection with the concepts of reliability and validity and in other chapters, but one or two are important to note here. One such is the field of research concerned with how constructs are differentiated and integrated. Bieri (1955) started the work on cognitive complexity and there have been a large number of studies since then. In 1966 he defined it as ' . . . the capacity to construe social behaviour in a multidimensional way. A more cognitively complex person has available a more differentiated system of dimensions for perceiving others' behaviour than does a less cognitively complex individual' (Bieri *et al.*, 1966, p. 185). Although originally related to theoretical considerations, it has now largely taken on a life of its own. (For detailed review see Adams-Webber, 1979).

What is problematic about this kind of work is its tendency to turn 'complexity-simplicity' into a trait, thereby ignoring the obvious — that we can move from complexity to simplicity and back, and we can be complex in one subsystem, say our view of cars, while being simple-minded in construing people (cf. Hall, 1966).

In the less-well-ploughed field of cognitive integration, we have Hinkle's (1965) demonstration that superordinate constructs not only have more implications than subordinate constructs, but they are also more resistant to change. To show this point, he de-veloped the Resistance-to-Change Grid. In this, the matrix con-sists of ticks indicating which constructs resist change in relation to which others. To obtain this matrix, subjects are presented with every possible pair of their constructs in turn and asked to look at each in terms of the preferred sides — for instance, *sympathetic-hard* and *reliable-unreliable*. They are asked to consider a situation in which they are compelled to change to the undesired pole on one of the constructs — they will either become a hard person or an unreliable person. A tick in the matrix indicates the construct on which they would prefer to remain unmoved. The more a construct resists change, the more superordinate it is likely to be.

Other workers have taken an interest in the extent to which people tend to use the extreme points on bipolar scales as opposed to the more central points. Some see the extremity ratings as indicative of maladjustment (e.g. Hamilton, 1968); others as a measure of personal meaningfulness of the scales (e.g. Landfield, 1968; Warr and Coffman, 1970; Bender, 1974). Bonarius (1971) offers the most sophisticated approach to the problem of interpreting extreme ratings by suggesting an Interaction Model. The extremity of the rating is a function of the interaction between three variables — the object (element) being rated, the person who does the rating, and the poles of the construct defining the scale. Some of the problems of the bipolarity assumptions in grids are spelt out by Yorke (1983).

Grids have been used to provide group data concerning the construing in specific areas of interest. For instance, if one wanted to investigate the effects of different room arrangements upon people's attitudes towards those rooms, then the grid elements might be pictures of the rooms with different furniture, lighting, shapes, wall surfaces and so on, which people would then be asked to construe (Honikman, 1976). In fact, many of the studies cited in this book concern group rather than individual findings.

Kelly tells us that, in certain respects, we can be construed as being alike: 'to the extent that one person employs a construction of experience which is similar to that employed by another, processes are psychologically similar to those of the other person (commonality corollary). For instance, while saying that certain people suffering from thought disorder are similar in having 'loose' relationships between their constructs for construing other people, and showing this by comparing their scores on a grid with scores obtained from other groups of people, one is *not* saying that they are alike in all other respects — far from it.

Methodologically, the grid can be used either to investigate the individual or particular aspects common to many subjects without violating the theoretical assumption that we are all unique in certain other respects.

The concept of reliability

Kelly is reported as referring to reliability as 'a measure of the extent to which a test is insensitive to change' — no facetious comment this, but a logical deduction from his theory which sees living creatures as forms of motion. Mair (1964 and 1964a) has suggested that instead of expecting a measure to yield near-identical scores for the same subjects on all occasions, one should substitute the notion of predicting whether there should or should not be change. Our aim should be to understand the meaning of change, not to regard it as an irritating interference with the 'reliability' of our tests by an irresponsible subject — to be looked upon as 'error variance'.

The idea of a static mind is a contradiction in terms. We should focus on the meaning of change. But apart from the general debate in psychology on the meaning of the concept of reliability, there are specific problems when it is applied to grid methodology. There is no such thing as *the* grid. Given the many forms, contents and analyses for existing grids (and envisaging the many kinds to come which have not yet been invented), it is clearly nonsense to talk of *the* reliability of *the* grid. It is at least as stupid as talking about *the* reliability of *the* questionnaire. We would be bound to ask what questionnaire, in *what* area, administerd to *what* kind of subjects, under *what* conditions and analysed in *what* kind of manner.

That reliability coefficients can, indeed, be useful sources of information is shown by Bannister's work on thought disorder (Bannister, 1962a). Not only did people said to be thought disordered relate constructs as if each were a virtually separate dimension, but they were also inconsistent in their use of these construct dimensions on a second occasion. Some so-called normal subjects also seem to use constructs as near discrete entities, but they use them with relative consistency. Thus, degree of consistency shown on immediate retest was used as one of the scores in a test designed to identify this type of disordered thinking (Bannister and Fransella, 1966 and 1967).

In Fransella and Bannister (1977), we cite a range of studies examining directly or indirectly the reliability of a number of scores derived from grids and conclude:

> . . . not only are there many different measures to be derived from the grid but each measure can almost invariably be derived from grids which themselves have varying elements and constructs and which might be applied not only to varying individuals but to varying populations of individuals with varying modes of administration and with varying validational fortunes.
>
> It seems sensible, therefore, to regard 'reliability' as the name for an area of inquiry into the way in which people maintain or alter their construing and to estimate the value of the grid not in terms of whether it has 'high' or 'low' reliability but whether or not it is an instrument which enables us effectively to inquire into precisely this problem. (p. 91).

The concept of validity

One way of thinking about the concept of validity in relation to grid methods is to liken them to the chi-square statistic. This is a format in which data can be placed and which then reveals if there is pattern or meaning to the data. The grid is exactly like that. It is not a test. There is no specific content. So its validity can only be talked about in the sense that we can question whether or not it will effectively reveal patterns and relationships in certain kinds of data.

A grid is therefore very different from a questionnaire allegedly measuring, say, aggressiveness. With such a questionnaire it is reasonable to ask to what extent it correlates with other ways of measuring aggression. But grids do not measure traits or characteristics in this sense. Also, as with reliability, it makes no sense to ask what is *the* validity of *the* grid.

Kelly was prepared, in terms of personal construct theory, to equate validity with usefulness and increased understanding. However, since there are always alternative ways of looking at things, this does not rule out the more traditional style of validity study. One such study was reported by Fransella and Bannister (1967). By comparing the way subjects ranked people they individually knew in terms of *like I'd like to be in character*, and *like me in character* with the rankings by the same people on the constructs *likely to vote Conservative (Labour, Liberal)*, it was possible to predict fairly accurately how each subject would vote at the subsequent General Election.

A number of single case studies have suggested that construct relationships are meaningfully linked to what is known about that individual and that certain predictable patterns pertain. For example, Salmon (1963) on sexual identity; Fransella and Adams (1966) on the meaning of arson for an arsonist; Rowe (1971) on the unlikely improvement with treatment of a depressed woman in terms of how *she* construed her depression.

Also in the clinical setting, others have looked at groups of people. For instance, Norris and Makhlouf-Norris (1976) give examples of ways of defining the self in grid terms; Smail (1970) showed that neurotics have a tendency to produce fewer constructs which deal with psychological aspects of human behaviour; Ryle and Lipshitz (1975) studied changes in construing in a marital therapy setting; repeated grid measures of self-esteem and patterns of identification with parents have been shown to be significantly associated with aspects of mutual interaction within the group (Caplan *et al.*, 1975); Implications Grid scores related significantly with changes in disfluencies for a group of stutterers over a treatment period (Fransella, 1972); Ryle and Breen (1972) showed marked patterns of differences in the grids of normal and neurotic subjects.

The fundamental postulate of personal construct theory uses the term 'anticipate'. This was deliberate on Kelly's part as it carries implications beyond the more limited notion of prediction. It suggests we seek to understand in order to involve ourselves with our world and to act upon it. Ultimately, validity can be seen as referring to the way in which a mode of understanding enables us to take effective action. The 'us' who takes action may well be the subject completing the grid rather than its administrator. Kelly makes the distinction between prediction and action as follows:

> Accurate prediction . . . can scarcely be taken as evidence that one has pinned down a fragment of ultimate truth, though this is generally how it is regarded in psychological research. The accuracy confirms only the interim utility of today's limited set of constructs. Tomorrow's genius will erect new dimensions, open up unsuspected degrees of freedom, and invite new experimental controls.

And yet, however useful prediction may be in testing the

transient utility of one's construction system, the superior test of what he has devised is its capacity to implement imaginative action. It is by his actions that man learns what his capabilities are, and what he achieves is the most tangible psychological measure of his behavior. It is a mistake to always assume that behavior must be the psychologist's dependent variable. For man, it is the independent variable. (Kelly, 1969b, p. 33)

Self-characterisation

Kelly many times insisted that he would prefer to be remembered, if at all, not for the invention of the psychology of personal constructs but for 'Kelly's first prinicple'. This was the simple statement that 'if you don't know what is wrong with a patient, ask him, he *may* tell you'. It seems likely that out of this joke Kelly invented (and he was prone to invent things very fruitfully out of jokes) the technique of person assessment which he called *self-characterisation*. It is interesting that psychologists seem always to have been suspicious of the value of direct personal statements: They make their tests oblique so that what is being measured is obscured from the subject. They embed lie scales in their questionnaires on the assumption that we are deceiving creatures. Yet many of us might feel that we have something scientifically meaningful to say concerning ourselves and what we have been about (cf. Morris, 1977). Self-characterisation is a format which invites us to say something about ourselves.

The request is put in the following way:

> I want you to write a character sketch of [person's name], just as if he were the principal character in a play. Write it as it might be written by a friend who knew him very *intimately* and very *sympathetically*, perhaps better than anyone ever really could know him. Be sure to write it in the third person. For example, start out by saying '[Person's name] is . . .'

This wording was designed to reduce any threat to a minimum and to encourage an overall assessment of the person by himself in as objective a way as possible. The aim is to find out how the person structures their immediate world, how they see themselves in relation to these structures and the strategies they have developed to handle their world.

The following is a self-characterisation written by a patient in a psychiatric hospital:

Do you know Mr Smith John? I do not. Only the other day he was walking down Marvels Lane to work. He can certainly walk, I have known Mr Smith to walk for miles John, sometimes to save a sixpenny bus fare. When you meet him in the street, he does not say much to you if hardly anything, he always seems to be in a hurry to go wherever he is going.

Have you seen his paintings of landscapes and trees? When he first began to paint he used to walk through the woods making sketches of trees, you know he loves trees, sometimes more than people, we should stop to think sometimes about people but he seems to show more affection and love for things and places, anything that cannot hurt him back or take anything away from him. He spent hours in that cold bedroom of his painting and waiting for the paint to dry. But he told me that there were other attractions in the woods, besides drawing trees and try as he might not to, it was looking at courting couples lying on the grass. He told me he used to go home and masturbate himself at what he had seen, then he would feel this deep guilt which would destroy any creative art he had in him. He would come to hate the courting couples because it would destroy his concentration in the woods and the creative spirit he wanted to draw trees and landscapes, and you know John some of his pictures were sometimes lovely, he has sold some, but he mostly gave them away to the school where his children go because they wanted to show their teachers and say 'my Dad done that'.

There is also his music John have you heard him play the accordion, the will power that man must have to start playing the accordion at forty-three, but as was said before the love he gives to things is unbelievable. His wife told me that he is always sweeping up and tidying the house and that he hates to see the children make a mess in the home, sometimes he gets very annoyed if they disturb him when he is practising. But even with his music, he gets that tremendous sexual urge to go out again and do all those things he hates doing, then he is lost for music, painting and anything creative that is deep inside him. But you know John a man like him must always be doing something then he is happy. But you also know John when he is happy and contented and creating he is a most agreeable person to get on with, but if you hurt him, he is not and seems to lose control of his speech and say horrible and nasty things, which he does not mean. Well John I must go. If you see Mr Smith give him my regards.

Instead of rushing off to count the verb to adjective ratio or even number of threat to non-threat words, suppose we look in fairly direct terms at what the person has said. Perhaps we ought to pay particular attention to the opening statement of any self-charac-terisation, because it seems likely that a person might try to pinpoint some central issue, set the tone and announce his general purpose right at the beginning. Mr Smith began by asking a question of the psychologist: 'Do you know Mr Smith?' and im-mediately answered the question for himself: 'I do not'. We could take this as an announcement of what, in jargon terms, might be called an 'identity problem' and then consider if this is a reason-able statement of his central theme.

Truly, the rest of the self-characterisation describes a man isolated from other people to the point where they are a menace because they interfere with his understanding of things and love of things. If the construct theory assertion that we come to under-stand ourselves via our understanding of other people (sociality corollary) is valid, then it seems quite likely that this man would be a mystery to himself. Apparently he has tried to understand himself by staring at his own navel rather than accepting that we see ourselves reflected in the eyes of other people.

We might look at the sequence of statements to observe the contrasts that are being drawn. This is a man in a great hurry, so that he says nothing to you but speeds on by and yet, in relation to 'things', he will spend hours in that cold bedroom of his, waiting for the paint to dry.

We might note the sequence of cause and effect as it is under-stood by the writer. An innocent stroll in the wood to enjoy the painter's view of things causes you to see men and women loving each other which causes you to masturbate which causes you to feel guilt which destroys your creative capacity as a painter.

We might note any contradictions. We play the accordion not for anyone else, only for ourselves, because it shows our de-termination and competence. Yet however casually we sell or give away our pictures, we do note the reaction of others to them.

Kelly (1955) deals at some length with methods of analysing self-characterisations but suggests no methods for quantifying their content. A step in the direction of organising this mass of information in content terms is Landfield's manual for categorising constructs (1971). But perhaps the most significant feature of the invention of the self-characterisation is the recognition that individuals' views of themselves may be materially more worth our consideration as psychologists than the interpretation of our clever ink blots or their answers to the semi-relevant questions which we have concocted for our questionnaires (Fransella, 1980, Jackson and Bannister 1985).

Measurement and Theory

While many are using grid methods within the theoretical framework from whence it came, many others find it useful in its own right. The problem with this latter approach is that sometimes valuable time is wasted in trying to answer questions that, if the theory were used, would not be asked. One such grid-generated problem is the question whether elicited constructs are 'better than' supplied constructs. This ignores the point that, in construct theory terms, you cannot 'supply' a construct, you can only supply a verbal label to which the person may attach their own construct (their *discrimination*). Clearly, if you supply a verbal label within the native language of the person, they can make *something* of it. If you supply, what is for them, an outlandish verbal label, nonsense will result.

The history of psychology gives us some fearsome examples of the way in which a technique can get out of hand once separated from its theoretical base. The Rorschach is one example of how a technique can become an industry and a very select club. There is a danger that the grid may go the same way, principally because its very mathematical ingenuity attracts many psychologists to it. No doubt it is this aspect that has attracted much more attention to the grid and vastly less attention to the self-characterisation with its lack of arithmetic scoring method.

But we have tried to indicate that meaningful questions can be asked of such qualitative data and it is clear that Kelly regarded the data produced in the self-characterisation as essentially similar to that provided in a grid format. One major difference is that the self-characterisation elicits more superordinate constructs than does the triadic method. However, if Hinkle's laddering procedure is adopted, there is no reason to suppose that the two methods will differ in level of superordinacy of constructs elicited. But no formal study has been carried out to investigate this point.

The Measure of the Person

Kelly summarised the personal construct psychology view of the individual thus:

> What I think this view of man as the paradigm of the scientist — and vice versa — does mean is that the ultimate explanation of human behavior lies in examining man's undertakings, the questions he asks, the lines of inquiry he initiates, and the strategies he employs, rather than in analyzing the logical pattern and impact of the events with which he collides. Until one has grasped the nature of man's undertakings, he can scarcely hope to make sense out of the muscular movements he observes or the words he hears spoken. In dealing with human behavior we inevitably find ourselves confronted with the human ingenuity it expresses. And that is the point of confrontation at which most psychology breaks down. (Kelly, 1969b, p. 16)

Perhaps our signal failure as psychologists to measure psychological aspects of the person derives from our habit of asking them to answer *our* questions rather than noting the nature of the questions which *they* are asking.

A change to a psychology of the inquiring person might additionally guard us from the danger of trying to turn our *descriptions of* ourselves into *prescriptions for* ourselves. Our own public faith in the tests which quantify and categorise people and our desire to show we are of some use have led us to design instruments for the disposal of people rather than for their and our enlightenment and understanding. Leman (1971) stresses:

> What I want to suggest here, is that many scientific theories (and not least some of those contrapted by psychologists) are not up to much as explanations of past events but are highly significant as programmes for future events of a kind to suit the originating scientist.
>
> (Something of the same sort goes on in advertisements: if you say, or show, that all considerable people are seen alive with your product, you are not reporting this as a fact recorded by the angel, you are trying to make it happen. You may remember the whisky poster which said nothing but 'Haig in

Every Home'.) . . . What I have been saying, is that I don't believe learning theory is correct as an explanation of things that have happened, of what you and I did yesterday, or last time a psychologist happened to be looking; that I think learning theory assumes, not man as he is and has hitherto been, but the ideal type of mechanarchic man; it doesn't really say what you are like, it says what They (namely, *hypocrite lecteur*, Us with Our hat on) would like you to be like; and that's fair warning that they will make you like that if they can.

Everybody capable of entertaining the thought now knows that psychology is a branch of politics, mainly concerned with disposal of bodies and the dispensing of existence: who is right, who wrong; who is to get the schooling and subsequent gravy; who not?

All through human history we have been subject to attempts (ranging from massive experiments by Genghis Khan and Nero to the work of Torquemada and Himmler) to make us jump to a punishment and reward schedule. Psychologists are finding it increasingly difficult to be non-aligned on this issue. We hope that Kelly's mathematical solution to the problem of perceiving pattern in the way in which people see their universe will not be distorted and completely absorbed into the traditions of psychological testing and used in terms of the assumptions underlying such testing. If the grid method is divorced from its theoretical base, this could well happen.

4 THE DEVELOPING PERSON

Larry and I had a conversation about hunting during which I mentioned that pygmies used darts dipped in poison for hunting and for defence. This intrigued Larry. Half an hour later he approached me with a stick and jabbed it into my leg.

'There, Don, she's dead.'

I slumped over, playing my part in the game. Larry became very excited and shouted:

'Let's bury her, Don!' As he tried to pick me up I collapsed on the floor and Larry started shovelling imaginary sand on top of me. Sally came into the room and, finding me 'dead', threw her arms around my neck and started to cry. I reassured her, and then noticed Larry curled up on the floor behind me.

'I wonder what you are doing?'

'I'm just lying here feeling sorry for you, Mrs Upton.'

(Kelly, 1970a)

People interpret and re-interpret themselves and their situation. The whole of personal construct psychology is based upon this fundamental idea that a person's psychological processes are channelled by the ways in which he or she successively construes events. Viewing the individual in relation to a time-line, changing from moment to moment, probably never absolutely the same from one second to the next, is an unusual vision in psychology. It accepts that since everyone is 'developing' or changing from the moment they are born, they can indeed be seen as a form of motion. If we follow this line of thought, then it becomes less meaningful to divide people up into arbitrary 'stages of development' such as childhood, adolescence, adulthood and old age; or, within the childhood bracket, oral, anal, genital and so forth.

A person in psychotherapy, as discussed later, is just as much involved in personal development as is the child. So are those in modern industrial settings when faced with great change. Staff and management in a large organisation involved in changing their internal structure and approach to customers may face the need to develop new personal strategies and ways of construing which, in turn, require core role reconstruing. For instance, many managers who pride themselves on being good at their job, construe this as involving the giving of clear instructions, making sure staff have a constant flow of information to pin on the notice-board and being seen to work hard. Such a manager may think that part of his success lies in the fact that he lets his staff get on with the job and may well regard too much personal 'closeness' as counter-productive, even weak. This manager faces massive threat when his organisation enforces a new style of management which focuses on staff involvement in decision-making, regards communication as a two-way process, and generally adopts a caring approach to staff. Dealing with this so that he can move on requires as much development as anything facing the average child.

And what of George Kelly himself? Zelhart and Jackson (1983) outline some of the environmental influences in his early life as a psychologist which could have played a part in the development of his theory. Going back even further in time, Fransella (1983) suggests some of the ways in which concepts Kelly was learning in his physics degree seem to have influenced the development of his ideas to be found in his later theory.

But, of course, developmental psychology still largely focuses on systematic changes a child undergoes along a time-scale and is not about the development of the businessman or George Kelly or most of the readers of this book.

Salmon (1970) points out how psychological theorising about stages through which a child develops — and other aspects of the child — has had a profound influence on the way in which parents have brought up their children; behaviourism led to rigorous time-tabling of living, everything metered according to a schedule; Freudianism led to an anxious concern about the probable harmful effects if the parent did not adopt the 'proper' emotional stance towards the child. Today parents have, perhaps, less guidance from the 'experts' on how to bring up their children.

Now it is the turn of teachers to be influenced by psychological theory. Piaget's theory of cognitive development in the child is having profound effects on teaching methods. Kelly and Piaget have much in common, including the conviction that human beings should be regarded as, say, 'thinkers' rather than 'organisms' or 'computers' or entirely bound by their 'unconscious dynamics'. Both argue that if we listen credulously to what people (children or adults) say, then we may start to understand why they approach life in the way they do.

It was a great misfortune that Kelly died before he made more explicit his view on the early development of the construing system. Many of the examples Kelly uses in his major work are to do with the construing of children. But no comprehensive application of the psychology of personal constructs to the development of construing systems is yet available, although beginnings can be seen in Jackson and Bannister (1985). We are thus left with the statement that the range of convenience of the existing theory potentially encompasses the construing of the child and the ways in which this construing changes with the years.

Since constructs are discriminations between events within a personal environment, some will and some will not have verbal labels attached to them. The rat at a choice-point in a maze may be seen as having cognitive maps *à la* Tolman (1932), or as having a construct about which way to turn in order to find water to quench its thirst. Having construed certain aspects of the choice-point in terms of smell, lighting — or whatever it is that rats construe at their choice-points — it anticipates that, by turning right, it will find water. It then tests out this anticipation by behaving — that is, by turning right — and what lies at the end of the path validates or invalidates its construing. In passing, it is interesting to note that Tolman used the term 'hypothesis' (borrowed from Krechevsky, 1932) for the expectation the animal develops in relation to a situation. These hypotheses are weakened if unconfirmed (invalidated) or strengthened if confirmed (validated).

Thus the study of rats, cats and apes comes well within the range of convenience of personal construct psychology, as indeed does the foetus. It is a foetal discrimination between an oxygenated and an oxygen-starved environment that precipitates it into being a 'child'. It is not argued that a foetus or young child recognises (in the sense of being able to verbalise) differences and similarities, but that its discrimination is not fundamentally different from that evinced by adults when we ask them to tell us which two of the sound of a fog horn, a siren and a penny whistle are alike and thereby different from the third.

Piaget

Many of Piaget's experiments showing the development of the concepts of time, number or movement can be seen as examples of how the child may develop the ability to construe certain events in the way others in the culture construe them. That is, how they acquire a superordinate construction about, say, the conservation of mass. Piaget's constructs about the stages through which a child psychologically evolves are derived from conventional discourse about reasoning and logic: concrete, formal, egocentric, reciprocal and so forth. They can be transformed into construct theory terms so that reciprocality equals the development of role construing, while concretism equals the use of subordinate constructs with only simple and inflexible links to superordinates, e.g. *ice cream* versus *no ice cream* implies *good* versus *bad*.

Recently we were given the opportunity to see an even closer resemblance between the Piagetian and Kellyian view. In his book *The Grasp of Consciousness* (1977), Piaget gives research evidence to illuminate the way in which unconscious (preverbal) aspects of a child's life become conscious:

> It would even seem that cognizance (consciousness) involves more than the incorporation of a new bit of information into an already established field (with all its characteristics) of consciousness. There is a genuine construction, which consists in elaborating not 'the' consciousness as a whole, but its different levels — that is, its more or less integrated systems. (Piaget, 1977, p. v)

After a description of a number of ingenious experiments to demonstrate this transition, he sums up by saying:

> . . . no one has contributed more than Freud to make us consider the 'unconscious' a continually active dynamic system. The findings in this book lead us to claim analogous powers for consciousness itself. In fact, and precisely insofar as it is desired to mark and conserve the differences between the unconscious and the conscious, the passage from one to the other must require reconstructions and cannot be reduced simply to a process of illuminations. (Piaget, 1977, p. 332)

There can be little doubt that whoever finally builds a theory of child development within the framework of personal construct psychology will want to use many of Piaget's experimental results as some of its bricks.

Yet, in spite of the many theoretical similarities between the two approaches, there are also some fundamental differences. For example, a personal construct psychologist would see the stages of development described by Piaget as related to experience (serial reconstruction) and not to age. She or he would also seek to construe and measure changes in structural rather than culture-content terms.

Salmon points out more fundamental differences between the two theorists, particularly in the divergence of their underlying philosophical assumptions:

> Piaget's theoretical account rests on an absolute view of truth. Assimilation, one half of the adaptation process, is defined as shaping outer reality to the inner conceptual world, while accommodation, the other half, represents a modification of the inner world to fit the demands of outer reality. Underlying such an account is the assumption that a person can directly experience pure reality and can distinguish between this and his inner conceptual world. This view runs counter to the philosophical basis of construct theory, whereby reality can never be known in any final, absolute way, but only through our constructions which, as a result of the varying validational outcomes of the behavioural experiments we make, are subject to continual revision. (Salmon, 1970, p. 214)

O'Reilly (1977) has pointed out that Piaget's construct 'egocentrism' is truly at odds with the personal construct standpoint. For Kelly, true egocentrism is not a possibility — from a very young age a child is seen as capable of sharing constructions and thus is behaving socially. But where Piaget is truly Kellyian is in pointing out that the child's view of the world is of vital importance in our understanding of that child's psychology. He tackled the problem of the child's self-awareness by asking the children to describe their thoughts on certain activities, such as walking on all fours, solving problems and so forth, rather than imposing meanings on them.

Personal Construct Approaches To Development

Salmon (1970) further points out that Piaget's theoretical model is primarily concerned with the development of thinking about the physical world and has relatively little to say about the development of the person *qua* person. She suggests that the development of personality in the child might be explained in terms of the Kellyian view of role. The child's construing of the mother's construct system is the jumping-off ground for the development of its own construing system. Children start out with this and use it in their dealings with others. Soon they meet others like themselves and find that all the anticipations they make do not always work out. So they develop new role constructs in relation to others of their own age and gradually elaborate and extend their role construing.

Perhaps the traditional Freudian Oedipus complex can be seen in the light of the child reaching an age when father expects his son to construe some of *his* constructs. The child may find that some of his father's constructs conflict with those developed in relation to his mother and so he shows hostility by 'acting the baby', or by aggression — he actively elaborates his system so as to incorporate some of his father's constructs. Development can be seen as occurring largely when anticipations fail. The over-protected child may never be put into a position where his use of the constructions his mother puts on events leads to invalidation. In this sense he fails to develop as an individual.

Shotter (1974) also sees development in social terms. For him there is a period of psychological symbiosis during which the mother sees her baby's behaviour as having meaning — it is construing — and she attempts to interpret what it is that the baby intends by its behaviour. But she also has intentions, things she wants her baby to do. Thus the baby gains access to the world through the mother who, in her turn, uses her understanding of her baby's intentions or desires to attain her own desires. With child and mother acting together, the child starts to single out aspects of the environment as distinct from the pair of them, and later to single out its mother as different from others, and eventually to single out itself as different from her.

Shotter cites some work of Lock to indicate the sort of investigation into child personality development that might stem from this approach. Lock (1976) reports some observations and interactions with a young child between 239 and 289 days old. Up to 258 days, the baby will not wave its arms about to another person with the intention of communicating, but with the intention of making something happen again. He says that 'because I was able to construe R's actions as being equivalent to meaning "Do that again" I was able to make his actions effective'. But at 289 days when a ball rolls out of its reach, the baby looks at Lock and waves its arms and then looks at the ball. Lock gives it back and the baby goes on playing quietly. Lock had now treated the baby's actions as if it were communicating and the arm-waving was a sign they had developed between them — meaning 'I want it again'.

Relevant to this discussion of mother-child interaction is the work of Davis (1979). He has studied the ways in which the mother's subsystem of constructs to deal with anticipating her child's behaviour is related to the ways in which she *actually* behaves towards that child. By far the most surprising result is the difference between mothers of male and female children. For the former there are no relationships between measures of construing and behaviour, whereas for the latter there are. Of course, it must immediately be stressed that these results can be discussed only in terms of the constructs and methods of measurement used in this study. Bearing that proviso in mind, Davis found that baby girls who are construed as having problems have mothers who are less likely to laugh, touch the baby affectionately or praise her. These mothers are, however, more likely to comment on their children's behaviour, imitate the babies and play with toys to which the babies are already attending. It can be argued that here the mother is not accurate in perceiving the meaning the child is intending to convey and so is invalidating her efforts at communication, as perhaps is indicated by the fact that the mother also 'interferes' with the toys the baby is playing with. Kelly's sociality corollary is an implicit comment on the tendency of those mothers of 'problem' children to imitate their babies. A relationship stems from construing the other person's constructs, not copying them in a ritual manner. Salmon (1979) also emphasises the importance of looking at 'children as social beings'.

In 1972, Fransella postulated that early development of some forms of behaviour, generally construed by society as abnormal, could be usefully studied from a personal construct psychology viewpoint. For instance, if a child's construing develops as it construes the construction processes of its mother, and as those of the child are construed by her, then we come near to the explanation of stuttering propounded by Johnson (1942). His theory was that most children have some form of speech disfluency as they learn to talk, but that a child will only become a stutterer if its parents are particularly concerned about its disfluencies and come to construe their child as a stutterer. In construct theory terms, we have the child looking at and organising its world largely through the eyes of its mother. This mother is, for some reason, concerned about speech and the disfluencies exhibited by her child. The child then comes to construe its own speech in terms of 'concern'.

The child's discriminations concerning speech will be largely pre-verbal and of a tentative nature. It will try out different ways of speaking — such as slowly, trying to get it all out in a rush, taking a deep breath, and so forth. It will observe the effects of these experiments on the mother and modify its speech according to the reaction perceived. What might be happening here is that the child is developing a network of constructs and implications to do with its speech. It follows from this that the stuttering child should have far more constructs to do with the speaking situation than the child who is not called a stutterer. It is argued that the thing that keeps a child stuttering is its inability to construe its *fluencies* and so it never comes to construe itself as a normal speaker.

Proctor and Parry (1978) say that Kelly's is an individualistic psychology and that he pays limited attention to the social context within which we develop. This is true in part. Kelly's emphasis is here, as always, on what we make of the situations in which we find ourselves. They are right in thinking that there is still some way to go before we can answer the question 'where do constructs come from?'. Always assuming that this is a useful question to be asking in the first place.

The Developing Construct System

Salmon (1970) considers that one of the major aspects of a developing construct system is the increasing degree of organisation of the system in terms of superordinacy. But there is little evidence on the specific processes that take place during the hierarchical development of construct systems. One of the difficulties experienced concerns measurement. There is no one operational definition of superordinacy. In 1967, Bannister and Salmon reported an experiment in which they compared ten measures. There were marked discrepancies. In commenting on this study, Bannister and Mair (1968) state: 'Until the various operational definitions of major constructs of the theory are more carefully derived from an examination of the logic of the theory, confusion is likely to increase' (p. 206). There is no indication that the position is any clearer more than 17 years later.

What little information there is suggests that children move from using physicalistic constructs to psychological ones (Little, 1968) and that psychological constructs increase in complexity or differentiation with age and become more integrated into a hierarchical system.

In one such study, Brierley (1967) elicited constructs from 90 boys and girls from working- and middle-class homes at ages 7, 10 and 13. She categorised the constructs in the following ways:

1. Kinship, e.g. *these are not in our family*.
2. Social role, e.g. *these are children*.
3. Appearance, e.g. *these are on the skinny side*.
4. Behaviour, e.g. *these play musical instruments*.
5. Personality, e.g. *these are nosey*.
6. Literal, e.g. *these have the same Christian name*.

Table 4.1 shows how the percentage of these categories varied across ages.

Table 4.1: Percentage of Six Types of Construct Elicited From Children in Three Age Groups

Type of construct	Percentage at age		
	7	10	13
Kinship	2.9	2.7	1.3
Social role	29.5	26.9	8.8
Appearance	32.3	30.6	8.9
Behaviour	24.3	31.0	41.3
Personality	9.8	18.4	39.7
Literal	0.2	0.0	0.0

Source: Brierley (1967)

Both behavioural and personality constructs increased in number with age and all others decreased except for kinship constructs, which showed no variation. Personality constructs showed the greatest increase. In general, at age 7, children were using kinship and social role constructs, at 10 appearance and behaviour constructs and at 13 personality constructs. A breakdown into sex groups showed that girls used appreciably more personality constructs than boys. At the age of 13, girls were more often using personality constructs in preference to all other kinds, while boys were more often using behaviour constructs. Dividing the children up on the basis of social class indicated that working-class boys were using more personality constructs than middle-class boys at ages 10 and 13, and working-class girls more than middle-class girls at age 10.

Applebee (1975, 1976) looked at the differentiation and organisation of the construct systems of samples of 6-, 9-, 13- and 17-year-old boys and girls in comprehensive, junior and infant schools. He used several grid measures of aspects of construct structure and found a complex, rather disorganised picture. In very general terms, it seems that as they grew older the children were able to discriminate more between people, used more constructs and more 'shades of grey'. The younger children seemed to construe things as being either black or white, good or bad. However, there was not a great deal of difference in degree of organisation as the children grew older.

Honess (1979) carried out a very detailed analysis of construct relationships in the implications grids of 203 children of ages ranging from 8 to 14 years. He found there was increased differentiation (complexity) of the construct system with increasing age. There was also some integration within the system at all ages. That is, the more superordinate the constructs the more implications those constructs have for the child, which is directly in line with Hinkle's original findings (1965).

Honess reports some interesting differences between the boys and girls. The changes in integration with increased age were due mainly to changes occurring in girls. He also found that boys have significantly more implications for constructs to do with activities and abilities and girls have more to do with constructs concerned with interpersonal relationships. If we interpret number of implications to indicate meaning, then these findings are themselves meaningful and in line with other studies on sex differences (cf. Fransella and Frost, 1977). Thus it seems that girls start to think about themselves and others at an earlier age than do boys and see such constructs as more important. This is given additional support by the finding of Bannister and Agnew (1977) that girls developed perceptions of themselves at an earlier age than boys.

The child's construing of self

Although there is a growing psychology of self and the 'self concept' there has been relatively little exploration of how, in childhood, we develop a notion of ourselves as individuals, as separate from others. Bannister and Agnew (1977) investigated the way in which children come to recognise themselves as distinct individuals as they increase in age. They attempted this by seeing at what ages (5-, 7- and 9-year-old) boys and girls came to recognise their own tape-recorded answers to questions four months after they had made them. By way of clues used, the younger children made most use of simple memory or whether they agreed or disagreed with the statements or whether they themselves undertook the activities described in the statements. As children grow older they seem to refer more to the kinds of likes and dislikes expressed in the statement (as indicating whether or not they have made the statement) and also considered its general psychological appropriateness to themselves. Thus a young child might claim a statement as his because the maker of the statement played football and he played football. This is quite a way from the construing of an older boy (age 9) who disowned (correctly) the statement 'I want to be a soldier' because he felt that since he could not bring himself to kill anyone he would have been unlikely to have expressed an ambition to be a soldier.

In answer to the general question 'how do we become different from others?' the 5-year-olds hadn't a clue (as they put it). The 7-year-olds seemed to favour some sort of trait/genetic theory that we are all born different and the 9-year-olds were beginning to work with the idea that it is different experiences which make us different or even beginning to toy with the cyclic notion of experience creating differences which in turn made for further different experiences. Interestingly, in the same study, when adults were asked to recall their first experience of sensing themselves as individual, as separate in some way, they often recounted the experience of loneliness, failure and rejection by others as sources of their sense of their own individuality.

The overall results of the study were in line with Kelly's argument that our construing of ourselves is developed as a bipolar construct of 'self *versus* others' and that the whole construct elaborates in the same way, and as part of, the system whereby we construe the world at large. Mancuso (1979) uses this construct to explore the characteristics of a parental reprimand; the child's constructions are at variance with the parents'.

Pupils and Teachers

A major piece of research has recently been reported by Salmon and Claire on classroom collaboration (1984). They studied the personal meanings teachers and pupils brought to the learning situation in four classrooms within two schools. The schools were inner city, mixed and multi-ethnic and were committed to mixed ability teaching. They studied many aspects of the classroom situation including racial conflicts, gender stereotyping, pupil-teacher as well as the children's own relationships. One of their main conclusions was: 'If there is a single message from this study, it must be that the cognitive and the social in school learning are inextricably intertwined.'

Other researchers have focused more specifically on teachers' and pupils' perceptions of each other and speculated on the possible effects of these. Nash (1973) carried out one of the early studies designed to look at that most difficult of subjects — how teachers' perceptions of children affect those children. An example of the sort of finding he reports is that teachers at the schools investigated appear to be sexist. According to grid results, the female teachers very definitely favoured girls in coeducational schools. He also related behaviour of children to teachers' perceptions of them and found that children in classes where they were perceived favourably by the teacher behaved differently from the way in which they behaved in classes where teachers viewed them unfavourably. For instance, Helen was perceived as *well-behaved* by one teacher and a *nuisance* by another. With the former there were no reports of unruly behaviour yet with the latter there were many. Whether there is a causal relationship here has yet to be determined. Conversely, Nash (1976) was concerned to show that children have expectations about teachers' behaviours, and that these expectations also influence behaviour. When a teacher behaves in a manner contrary to such expectations, there can be classroom strife.

Hargreaves (1977) has been severely critical about these and other studies on the grounds of small samples and, in particular, methodological weaknesses. For instance, he points out that when constructs elicited from teachers are not related to any specific context, the teachers may be using those constructs differently. The underlying assumption is that 'all significant typifications are necessarily *transcontextual*, and that the test can tap the constructs on a context-free basis'. But clearly the classroom is itself a *social context* within which a teacher's superordinate constructs (personal values) must be examined (as demonstrated by Salmon and Claire, 1984).

More recently, Rosie (1979) has reported another study on interpersonal relationships in the classroom, but this time from the point of view of how pupils construe pupils and how teachers construe teachers; and Beveridge (1982) has been more concerned with interpretations of young children's language than the social context, but also within a classroom setting.

Humphris (1977) was interested in how disadvantaged young children perceived themselves and how they were perceived by teachers. She studied a group of six 4-year-old boys identified by teachers as having speech problems and compared them with six having no such problem. The speech-disordered children did not see themselves as being any different from the other boys in the class (in terms of the constructs used), yet the teachers construed them more unfavourably than the other boys. Of particular interest is the fact that the dimensions along which the two groups were construed by the teachers were different. It was not just that one group was *lazy* and *stupid* and the other *industrious* and *clever*. The 'normal'-speaking children were considered along the dimension defined by *happy, warm, participates easily, communicates easily with me*, with the second dimension defined by the construct *cooperative*. However, those children seen by the teachers as having speech problems were seen first in terms of *not being warm*, then as being *happy, not enjoying doing things with others, not being cooperative and as being unaware of others*. Happy in their isolation. In fact, every loading on the first component was in the negative direction.

In terms of this study, these two groups of small boys were seen by their teachers differently. The happy 'normal'-speaking child is warm, participates and communicates easily. But the disfluent unhappy child is seen as isolated and, most importantly, uncooperative. Logically, the 4-year-old boy with speech problems would have to be unhappy to be seen as cooperative by the teacher.

Findings such as these, if replicated, have important implications for teacher-training and much work is being carried out from various standpoints to increase our understanding of what helps make a good teacher.

Pope (1978) suggests that student teachers should be given feedback concerning the changes taking place in their personal construing during training as well as feedback on their academic progress. In her study she found that most change in construing took place in the early part of the course and that, by the end of the course, the students had somewhat reverted to their former position. The model teachers have of themselves, their task and their pupils cannot but be a vital factor in the educational process. Pope and Keen (1981) outline many of the studies that have been carried out in the field of educational psychology.

A somewhat different approach to the study of classroom settings was adopted by Micklem (1978). He was interested in the meaning of silence for those children who fail to contribute to class discussions. Such silent children cause unease in many teachers. It is often construed by them in terms of personality — they are cold or unassertive or both; or in terms of general social inadequacy; or as indicating a deep-seated neurotic condition. To look at how the children, as opposed to the teachers, construed it, Micklem inquired, in grid terms, how both 'silent' and 'talking' children saw themselves and how they saw each other. There was good agreement amongst the children as to who was silent and who outspoken in the class, and the two groups used the constructs in the same way. However, the outspoken children did not sit near to, nor have much to do with, the silent members of the class. But in spite of this the silent members did not see themselves as being apart from the outspoken group. Further study of such a discrepancy in social relationships and self-perceptions could well be important in helping the ostracised child.

Personal Development and the Educational System

Educational growth is not the accumulation of more and more pieces of information, but the development of an increasingly complex structure for organising and interrelating ideas. If this notion were followed, then some of the traditional boundaries between 'subjects' at school would cease to exist (consider an English Literature-History-Current Affairs-Geography merger). The present system favours the development of the dread disease, referred to by Kelly as 'hardening of the categories', rather than the elaboration of a network of meanings.

Thus personal construct psychology has implications for the educational process itself. Children being taught arithmetic are shown methods for dealing with numbers in certain ways so as to get certain types of answer. They then move on to another subject, say, algebra, to learn other ways of dealing with numbers. But what of children who have found that arithmetical procedures are quite adequate for solving all the problems with which they have been presented? If at the end of their arithmetic course they had been presented with problems with which their arithmetic construing system could not deal, the experience of invalidation might have encouraged them to view algebra as a salvation rather than a pointless exercise. The experience of being 'wrong' is educationally as important as the experience of being 'right'.

It may be that the whole developmental cycle is best maintained as a continuous movement by alternating the experiences of validation and invalidation. Bannister (1965a) found that people tend to tighten the relationship between constructs when they experience validation and loosen when invalidated. Elaboration occurs when constructs are sufficiently loosely related to deal with new experiences. This has been demonstrated recently by Fürst (1978).

Kelly argued that elaborating the way a person understands and interprets the world is achieved by alternating between tight and loose construing as described in the Creativity Cycle. When we construe tightly, our constructs are closely related and well articulated and our expectations are specific and concrete. When we construe loosely, our constructs are vaguely related and only partly verbalised and our expectations are broad and approximate. Thus we range between 'facts and dreams'. A few brass tacks rescue us from schizophrenia — yet a fantasy or two safeguards us from obsessionality. Neither tight nor loose construing is good in itself — development is a word for movement between the two.

That loose-to-tight construing is a normal, if submerged, aspect of education, is indicated by the work of Runkel and Damrin (1961). They showed that teacher-training students who were at the beginning of training (measured in terms of their mastery of the subject) were using a multiplicity of loosely related dimensions in terms of which to view children. At a mid-point in training, students had narrowed down to a simple tight view using only a few dimensions. Towards the end of training, the students again loosened their subsystems. Success as a teacher seemed to relate to the distance moved from loose-to-tight rather than to being solely at one or the other. This topic is further explored in Adams-Webber and Mirc (1976).

Children With Problems

One of the many problems encountered by teachers is that of children who are not learning to read as they should. Many teachers seek the explanation for such failure in defects of the children and not in their interaction with home and school (Ravenette, 1968). The most popular explanation given by teachers in Ravenette's study was that of lack of intelligence, which tends to imply that there is little that can be done. Ravenette reports how Kelly was once asked how his theory related to the problem of a child failing to learn to read and how he replied 'find out if the child likes the teacher'. Such an answer suggests changing the emphasis from 'why is the child not *able* to read?' to 'why does the child not *want* to read?' An investigation of how the child views the school and home environment and his or her idea of what reading is about may provide explanations of the child's reluctance to do what others do.

For example, a child may have experienced persistent failure — perhaps at nursery school, perhaps in relation to an elder, clever brother, or his parents' expectations — and come to see himself as a failure. Having construed himself as a failure (either generally or more specifically in relation to reading), there must be some problematical implications for him in being a success. Ravenette points out that the implications of success are likely to be very important and need to be identified if progress is to be made. They may relate to another personal dimension potentially troublesome to the child — that of growing up — and learning to read is part of growing up. Perhaps his perception of adult life has not been a happy one and he has witnessed cruelty and unhappiness which makes adulthood look an undersirable state.

Ravenette suggests that in addition to finding out if the teacher or parent likes the child, one should look to see if either is trying to force the child into a role which it does not see as appropriate. If this happens, the child is being denied the means of developing its own personal identity. Ravenette sees the classroom situation in terms of the sociality corollary (that is, concerned with construing the construction processes of others), and links it with hostility (extorting validational evidence in favour of a type of social prediction which has already proved itself a failure).

> When children and teachers continue to maintain their own constructions of each other, in the face of continued interpersonal difficulties, we see this as hostility in the classroom. When a teacher can abandon, if only for a limited time, his existing constructions of his problem children he may provide room for growth for each of them, and for himself. When a child, if only for a limited time, can become aware of his own constructions of himself and others, he too may enjoy a breathing space in which more harmonious relationships can develop. Kelly, through personal construct theory, invites the psychologist to reconstruct *his* role in such a way as to help him to promote just those kinds of change. (Ravenette, 1977, p. 280)

Ravenette's approach to the whole area of children's problems is exemplified by his paper 'The exploration of consciousness: personal construct intervention with children' (1980).

Nash (1973) looked at 15 children who were in a remedial reading class. Not only were these children at the bottom of the class academically, but they were also perceived unfavourably by the teachers in personal terms. They were construed as dull, less capable, troublesome, badly behaved and also passive, stolid, immature and less interesting. So not only are these children seen as having low ability but also as having certain undesirable personality characteristics and, perhaps most significant of all, as being less interesting. These findings are very similar to Humphris' (1977) results concerning children unskillful in speaking. Taken at face value, one can conclude that teachers do not like children who are seen as having problems with such skills as reading or speaking. This may be a self-fulfilling prophecy as the child may indeed come to dislike the teacher.

One of the common problems children have is being labelled 'delinquent' by adults. One or two studies have tried to find out how these delinquents construe their lives and those around them. For instance, at the time of being sent to a training centre, delinquents seem to lack identification with authority figures but identify strongly with their delinquent pals. But during the training period, they become more identified with authority figures and less with other delinquents.

Rather gloomy results are reported by Norris (1977). She studied the construing of young men in a detention centre and found that four-fifths of the boys left the centre with reduced aspirations, half of these had less favourable views of themselves and rule-breaking was considered less undesirable.

In a study designed to show differences between groups of delinquent boys, Holland (1971) had them fill out a questionnaire, once as themselves and again as other people might fill it out. The questionnaire was designed to measure 'powerlessness'. Some are of the opinion (e.g. Gold, 1969) that youths take part in delinquent acts as a reaction to feelings of powerlessness. This fits in with the idea that delinquents are more likely to identify with others of their own age than with authority figures. Holland found that the boys as a whole *did* see themselves as less powerful than people having high social status, such as doctors, policemen, school teachers and a prime minister. Less obvious was her finding that boys who abscond see these powerful figures as relatively *less* powerful than do non-absconders.

This is an example of what is meant in personal construct psychology by behaviour being seen as a question. Perhaps the behavioural question is 'What exactly is the extent of *their* power?' or 'Are *they* as lacking in power as I think they are?' Holland found a kind of realistic hopelessness in both groups of delinquents. They recognised the existence of a *pyramid* of power above them in that, for instance, they saw policemen as being relatively powerless. Policemen were also seen as believing that people 'can't change much'. If we come to believe that we cannot change no matter what we do, then presumably our behaviour must become repetitious indeed.

Others who have looked at the construing of 'delinquent' young people are Heather (1979) and Miller and Treacher (1981).

Weinreich has focused on adolescents with a different type of problem by studying self-image and identification in immigrant adolescents (1979; 1980). Conflict may arise when one identifies with someone who, at the same time, has certain qualities which one dislikes. One of his findings was that immigrant girls are better able to acknowledge conflicts of identification than boys, who are more likely to deny that there is any conflict.

Strachan and Jones (1982) have looked at changes in adolescents' identification in a more general context.

Young people who are emotionally disturbed are being studied in terms of the structure rather than the content of their construct systems. Reker (1974) postulated that the emotionally disturbed child has failed to develop an adequate interpersonal conceptual system for interpreting and anticipating his social environment. He found that disturbed boys had less differentiated construct systems to do with construing people, but did not differ from non-disturbed boys in this respect when construing inanimate objects.

In a more recent study, Hayden and Nasby (1977) looked at structure and process rather than content in a group of emotionally disturbed boys aged between 10 and 16 years. Their argument follows on from Bannister's in relation to thought disorder; i.e. construct systems that are lacking in structure make it difficult for the person to see meaning in social events (see pp. 142-50). It was therefore predicted that the lack of structure of the construct systems of emotionally disturbed boys would be related to adequacy of social adjustment.

The elements used to elicit constructs from each boy were photographs taken of another boy while he was working on a difficult task in an intelligence test. These photographs were used in a grid format so as to yield information on organisation of the boys' *ways* of construing. In addition, each boy was required to rank the photographs in the order in which he supposed they were taken. This latter procedure was derived from implications of the sociality corollary. The test-retest reliability of this prediction of photograph arrangement was 0.48 (p<.01). The authors did indeed find significant relationships between their boys' accuracy in construing the sequence of another's behaviour, their own behaviour and construct system structure. The more accurate they were, the more appropriate was their own behaviour in social situations and the more differentiated their own construct system. Those who were poor at person perception in this study

tended to interpret aspects of social events by using only one and the same side of the bipolar dimension as well as by using the less extreme ratings. In other words, these boys apply their interpersonal interpretations to events in a way that formulates the events as being functionally equivalent or renders them non-discriminative. (Hayden and Nasby, 1977, p. 319)

In a footnote, the authors report that, ten months after the study had been completed, there was no difference between the boys who improved in that time and those who had not improved in terms of original diagnostic classification. But there was a correlation of 0.70 between improvement and accuracy of construing the sequence of photographs.

Gordon (1977) studied another adolescent 'deviant' group — the profoundly deaf. The generally held view of the prelingually deaf person is that their linguistic limitations force them to see people in non-elaborated terms; that is, black or white, good or bad, warm or cold. Such construing is likely to give rise to a relatively unidimensional, undifferentiated structure in a grid. Gordon, in fact, found very little difference between the grid results of a group of deaf and a group of normal-hearing adolescents. The results suggest that deaf teenagers can 'organize in a sophisticated fashion' the few linguistic concepts they have at their disposal concerning the personal qualities they see in people.

One of the problems in dealing with the profoundly deaf is that of eliciting constructs. Baillie-Grohman (1975) approached this in an unusual way. She argued, and Gordon's results support her argument, that the deaf, with little or no language, nevertheless have relatively complex construct systems. However, she believes that the discriminations they make are more elaborate than they can express verbally. She therefore used facial expression, mime, gesture and signs to elicit constructs from a group of 14 deaf children. Having worked out a difference between two known people, each child was asked to mime that difference to the other children. The essence of the mime was then drawn by an artist and the drawing shown to the child and altered until it truly represented what the child wanted to convey. The other children were then asked to think of a person they knew who showed the behaviour represented in the mime. In this way a pool of constructs was elicited from the group and the children related them to people each knew in grid format.

Another so-called problem group are the subnormal. Yet low intelligence in a person should not preclude us from trying to see the world through their eyes and hence understand the meaning of their struggles to deal with it. Nor does it prevent us from using forms of grid to quantify such meanings, as the work of Barton and colleagues (1976) and Wooster (1970) suggest.

Development As A Perpetual Experiment

Reading, arithmetic, going to school, are new adventures for children. But the approach also states that children will only willingly embark on these adventures if they think the quests worth undertaking. In *Behavior is an Experiment* (1970a), Kelly describes a school which emphasises adventurousness in personal construct terms:

> The primary object of a good school is not to control behavior, or even to 'give' the child experience — two goals frequently cited by educators. In a society convinced that freedom is more than a happy personal convenience, that it also enables men to make the most of their capacity to help each other, a school cannot allow itself to become an instrument for keeping the under-privileged in line by squelching their impulses. Moreover, the school cannot permit itself to take the position that experience, instead of being a prerogative of all human life, is to be doled out in calculated amounts by the educational establishment. Yet none of this is to say that limits on behavior are to be abandoned or that experience cannot proceed in an orderly fashion.

The limits on behaviour are seen as largely self-imposed by the child,

> but regardless of who imposes them, they serve as guard-rails permitting freer experimentation within presumed limits of safety. Occasionally one finds the limits have been set altogether too far out and a child shrinks back from exploration. Sometimes they are set too close in and he explores coherently only within infantile orbits. When he must function outside the limits, his behaviourally posed questions are observed to be frantic and his experiments inconclusive. (Kelly, 1970a, pp. 261-2)

In order to take part in the child's experimentation, the teacher must get some idea of what is being seen through the child's eyes; he or she must 'enact a role'. Mrs Upton, the head of the school, sees fantasy play as one of the ways in which children role-play parts that are beyond their present self-imposed limits. She actively participates in the games her children play and suggests experimental roles they might adopt that could lead to the elaboration of their construct systems.

This notion of the person as an experimenter seems eminently applicable to the so-called 'adolescent problem' — a problem *for* adults, not just *in* adolescence. They can be seen as experimenting, as actively elaborating their construct systems (showing aggression in the Kellyian sense). The question for the adults becomes one of 'why do they need to experiment so actively?'. If there were a different emphasis in our schools, each child might be enabled to ask their own personal questions, rather than simply be part of a standard class apparently asking the same questions.

As an example of the more extreme attitudes pervading our educational system consider these words from an open letter to MPs:

> The new fashionable anarchy flies in the face of human nature for it holds that children and students will work from natural inclination rather than the desire for reward.
>
> Exams make people work hard. Much opposition to them is based on the belief that people work better without reward and incentive, a naïveté which is against all knowledge of human nature. All life depends upon passing exams. If you fail at football, they drop you to the reserves. If you fail in business you go bankrupt. If you fail in politics, you are forced to resign (or, in some countries, get shot). To create an educational system without examination is to fail to prepare children and students for the realities of adult life. (Cox and Dyson, 1969)

Is it not against constructs like these that the adolescent is rebelling? They are challenging the premise that 'all life depends upon passing exams' and the pre-emptive view of human nature expressed above. They do not always see why life needs to be competitive — they may be experimenting with opting out of competition, and the answers they get from society will help determine what future questions they ask.

Development As Opera Not Overture

Personal construct psychology offers many new ways of thinking about development, that is, development in the traditional psychological sense of birth to adolescence. Since we are seen as being perpetual forms of motion, theoretically there is continuous development. But perhaps the word 'development' is misleading. It implies movement towards some end product, whereas there is no such concept within the psychology of personal constructs. It might be more productive to talk about personally meaningful 'change' instead. We are perpetually changing and, because we are biological creatures, some of the changes occur as each of us physiologically matures from conception to old age. So we have a theory of perpetual change, even though we sometimes ask questions of our environment that help us only to paint ourselves into a corner. This standpoint makes us think of the child as a person rather than as 'savage' or 'computer' or 'mini-adult'. It has implications for the education process itself, and it particularly emphasises the importance of the child's interpretation of its environment. It concerns us with the development of psychological processes rather than with arbitrary stages or traits. Lastly, it has implications for the child who is construed by society as having problems, be they 'educational' or 'personal' — remembering always that these are our categories and not the child's.

In a paper 'Social inheritance' written by Kelly in 1930 (see Stringer and Bannister, 1979), he was already emphasising the ludicrous aspects of the nature-nurture controversy and the reciprocal nature of the individual-society interaction. In a preface to 'Social inheritance' Bannister argues that 'it is through the personal meaning which we give to our education and the personal way in which we live it out, that we give back to our society that which we have created'.

5 PERSON TO PERSON

> . . . the Variations have amused me because I've labelled 'em
> with the nicknames of my particular friends — *you* are Nimrod.
> That is to say I've written the variations each one to represent
> the mood of the 'party' — I've liked to imagine the 'party'
> writing the variation him (or her) self and have written what I
> think they would have written — if they were asses enough to
> compose — it's a quaint idea and the result is amusing to those
> behind the scenes and won't affect the hearer who 'nose nuffin'.
> (Edward Elgar, letter to a friend)

Of all the many curious divisions in psychology, there is none so
strange as making a special case of 'social psychology'. Strange
because, unless one is a hermit, what one does takes place within a
social context. Even construing a person as being a hermit has a
social referent — being *not* social.

The Doctrine of Norms

Kelly set out the basis of a social psychology in the commonality
and sociality corollaries. Commonality is related to cultural issues
and sociality to role relationships. Although personal construct
psychology concerns itself with the construer, the commonality
corollary states that a number of individuals can have the same
constructions of experience. This does not mean that to construe
things similarly people must have had similar experiences. It
means they must construe their experiences in a similar way. We
can thus abstract certain common characteristics seen to exist in
certain groups of people and give the name 'cultures' to these
similarities and differences. Or we can descend from that very high
level of abstraction and perceive similarities and differences *within*
a particular culture.

Living in a similar culture, we come to share certain constructs with others of our group, though the implications of these constructs may not be identical — for construct systems are indeed *personal*. In a warrior culture, men do not necessarily agree as to the precise braveness or cowardliness of a particular act, but they do agree that the important aspect of many acts is their braveness-cowardliness content. To another culture that reveres, say, logical thinking, whether the person acts in a brave or cowardly way is relatively unimportant; the acts will be construed rather in terms of their logic.

'Culture' specifies the superordinate dimensions along which the acts of individuals are primarily construed. It dictates 'ideal' personality characteristics. For instance, not so long ago, in aristocratic sections of European society, personal honour was valued above all else and many died in its defence.

Cultural norms have considerable relevance in many aspects of life. For instance, they can underlie psychiatric diagnosis. A person may deviate from a group standard just so much before being pronounced 'mentally ill' if they are held to be suffering from some condition over which they have insufficient control; 'criminal' if they are held responsible for their behaviour; 'delinquent' if they are young but responsible; or 'neurotic' if they are behaving at the far end of the 'normal' range but are held not to be *totally* responsible. There are groups of people about whom society cannot make up its mind. For instance, 'mentally abnormal offenders' (Rollin, 1969) are seen to be mentally ill but also sometimes deemed to be responsible for their acts and so they are sent to prison on one occasion when they commit an offence and to a psychiatric hospital on another.

There are degrees of deviation as well. If a person is a 'little' mentally ill, they are likely to be still on the 'normal' continuum and thus may be described as 'neurotic'. But if their behaviour is beyond the cultural pale, they will be labelled 'psychotic'. Statistical norms are established for psychotics, for neurotics, for psychopaths, for delinquents. Of course, only the extreme cases are readily identifiable in terms of these normative categories. All that can usually be said normatively about most of us is that we are neither giants nor dwarfs, sinners nor saints.

In his book *Social Influence and Social Change* (1976), Moscovici argues that it is more productive to view the deviant, however classified, in positive rather than negative terms. The deviant is not someone who has failed to adapt to the social system, but is a potent force for bringing about social change. The personal construct psychologist would add to this view that the study of deviant groups as groups is unlikely to be a productive occupation unless one also focuses on the meaning deviance has for the individuals in such groups.

But, within any given social setting, there are of course certain expected attitudes and behaviours. We all have our own private set of norms (constructs) which lead us to expect certain behaviours and attitudes and, in turn, certain attitudes and behaviours are expected (and required) from each of us. Where personal construct psychology differs from the usual social psychological approach is in how it conceptualises attitudes and behaviours that deviate from the expected and the required. The explanation is sought not in the social process, but in the construing of the deviant or group of deviants or askers of nonconformist questions. We would seek to find out what questions the non-conformists are asking and what answers they are seeking by behaving in that particular way. Describing and categorising the behaviour is not sufficient. We need to know why it is being carried out in the first place.

The Person and the Community

Long before Kelly formalised his construing into the psychology of personal constructs, he wrote an essay, 'The social inheritance' (Kelly, 1930), in which he took up the theme that our construing, as individuals, is negotiated with those with whom we live. Not only with those with whom we *now* live. Our construing is influenced by those who have gone before us and who have bequeathed us our language, our customs and the consequences of their lives. Karst and Groutt (1977) took up this theme in a specific and fascinating way by living for a short time in a mystical religious commune in America and examining the superordinate constructs that informed the life of the commune. They culled these superordinates from the language — conversations, writings, stories and so forth — of the commune. For example, they elicited from seven individual members of the commune the following jointly held and used constructs (both emergent and contrast poles are given):

those who stand with me	versus	*those who deceive*
insider	versus	*outsider*
close friendship	versus	*merely together*
evidence of total belief	versus	*holding back*
companionship	versus	*solitude*
communicate with easily	versus	*communication only with difficulty*
companionship	versus	*sexual relationship*

It became clear from their examination that these constructs have a common theme and represent broadly the idea of the brotherhood community itself *versus* the outside world. Karst and Groutt went on to take up the issues implicit in that most basic of all constructs, *same* versus *different*. Clearly (see commonality corollary) we share the constructs of our communities, but as individuals we also differ in some respects from the common view. For example, one of the major superordinate constructs of the commune was *letting go* versus *holding on*. To *let go* is to become tranquil, to submit to the rule of the group, to attain perfect spirituality, while to *hold on* is to be trapped in the snares of the material world. However, they found one woman within the commune who increasingly saw the implications of *letting go* as *being swallowed up*, having your freedom limited and also experiencing plain ordinary boredom, while inevitably the contrast, *holding on*, was seen as about retaining choice. Not surprisingly she eventually left the commune.

One of the fundamental issues of commune (and possibly any community) life relates to the question of what purpose is the commune serving for the person, what aspect of his or her construction system does it validate. The implication of the work of Karst and Groutt is that there can be two diametrically opposed purposes served by living within a group which very explicitly shares and behaves according to common beliefs.

Joining a commune may be, for some, an act of aggression (the active elaboration of their construct system). It may represent adventure, experiment, exploration, literally going into a new world. For others it may be an act of hostility (the attempt to extort validational evidence for a kind of social construction which was already proving a failure). The commune may serve as a context in which to act out a pattern of beliefs which have proved invalid for the outside world; the hostile person may love the commune because his or her doubtful convictions about the nature of human kind are here necessarily true because they are *enforced* by the 'laws' of the commune. In the wider world outside their beliefs have been increasingly shown to be irrelevant or invalid. Our understanding comes not from calling these people deviant but by construing their construction processes.

The Experimenter and the Subject

Kelly saw the sociality corollary as providing a basis for a social psychology. It states that 'to the extent that one person construes the construction processes of another we may play a role in a social process involving the other person'. By understanding the way another person sees things, we can converse and engage in joint enterprises.

Few would argue that the traditional psychology experimental format (social or otherwise) sees experimenter and subject as engaging in a joint enterprise. In most cases the enterprise belongs exclusively to the experimenter. 'Introspections' from the subject are often asked for but rarely acted upon unless it is to improve the experimental design. This clearly denies the plain fact that the official psychological experiment takes place within a social setting. Even the rat performs differently if it has experienced social interaction, i.e. 'gentling', an academic way of saying that it has been handled and stroked (e.g. Levine, 1956).

The experimenter-subject dyad can be looked upon as an example of a role relationship; one in which the subject is desperately trying to construe the construction processes of the experimenter — 'just what *is* he after?' Rosenthal (1967) talks of effects that can occur between a male experimenter and his subject. *Biosocial* effects are shown in the findings that female subjects are smiled at 70 per cent of the time whilst males receive smiles on only 15 per cent of occasions; experimenters take more time to collect data from females than from males; young subjects are less likely to say 'unacceptable' things to older experimenters; blacks control their hostility more with white than with black experimenters.

Situational effects include the findings that responses obtained by experienced experimenters differ from those with less experience; and those who know the subjects get different results from those who test strangers. One of Rosenthal's best-known ideas is that of the 'experimenter bias effect'. That is the basic fact that in most research the experimenter has some expectations as to the outcome of the study. For example, in one of Rosenthal's own experiments, all experimenters were given the same instructions on how to carry out a study in which subjects judged the expressions on faces in ten photographs. Half the experimenters were told that previous research had shown the 'well-established fact' that people rated the photographs as those of 'successful' people, while the other group were told that judges tended to rate them as 'unsuccessful'. Experimenters who were led to expect that their subjects would judge the photographs to be those of 'successful' people did, in fact, obtain higher ratings of success compared with those of subjects whose experimenters expected them to see the photographs as portraying 'unsuccessful' people.

Rosenthal's category of *psychosocial* effects in experimenter-subject interaction, includes studies showing that 'researchers higher in status — a professor as compared to a graduate student, or a captain as compared to a corporal — tend to obtain more responses that *conform* to the investigator's suggestions: and investigators who are warmer towards people tend to obtain more *pleasant* responses'. Likewise, Hoffman and others (1970) found that people are more likely to sort photographs into emotionally positive categories with 'friendly' experimenters than they are when the same experimenters are 'neutral' in their manner.

In his paper 'On the social psychology of the psychological experiment' Orne (1962) quoted the following passage from Pierce, written in 1908:

> It is to the highest degree probable that the subject['s] . . . general attitude of mind is that of ready complacency and cheerful willingness to assist the investigator in every possible way by reporting to him those very things which he is most eager to find, and that the very questions of the experimenter . . . suggest the shade of reply expected . . . Indeed . . . it seems too often as if the subject were now regarded as a stupid automaton . . . (Orne, 1962, p. 779)

Orne describes how he asked some acquaintances to do the experimenter a favour by performing five press-ups and how they asked in amazement *why*? He asked another similar group of people to take part in a short experiment involving doing five press-ups and they asked simply *where*? There is a clearly defined social situation called 'taking part in an experiment' in which the specific roles of subject and experimenter are well understood and carry with them well-defined, mutual role expectations.

In a previous study (Orne, 1959) it was found that a particular experimental effect only occurred with those subjects who were able to state what the experimenter's hypothesis was.

> . . . it is futile to imagine an experiment that could be created without demand characteristics. One of the basic characteristics of the human being is that he will ascribe purpose and meaning. In an experiment where he knows some purpose exists, it is inconceivable for him not to form cues, no matter how meagre; this will then determine the demand characteristics which will be perceived by and operate for a particular subject. Rather than eliminating this variable then, it becomes necessary to take demand characteristics into account, study their effects, and manipulate them if necessary. (Orne, 1962, p. 778)

Work indicating that the psychological experiment is a social situation has been stressed here because it underlies the importance of reflexivity in psychological theory. It is necessary for psychologists to see themselves as part of the subject-matter of psychology. Personal construct psychology sees the psychologist and the subject as being in the same interpretative boat and helps break us of the habit of playing at being 'scientists' in the ritual and separatist sense of the term. When we talk of the subject understanding the experimenter's hypothesis, we are using Kelly's notion of *role*. Construing the construction processes of another in no way implies a common 'correct' understanding — there may be total mis-understanding — but our understanding of another's under-standing determines our subsequent behaviour. Kelly goes on to state:

> Here we have a take-off point for a social psychology. By attempting to place at the forefront of psychology the under-standing of personal constructs, and by recognizing, as a corollary of our Fundamental Postulate, the subsuming of other people's construing efforts as the basis for social interaction, we have said that social psychology must be a psychology of

inter-personal understandings, not merely a psychology of common understandings. (Kelly, 1955, p. 95)

This position offers us a potentially unifying concept between individual and social psychology.

Social Psychology

In the traditional social psychology experiment we are presented with the study of interactions between subjects rather than between experimenter and subject. Investigation is made of the attitudes of subjects, not the attitudes of the experimenter, though recent work has begun to stress the interaction between the two (Reason and Rowan, 1981). To indicate ways in which personal construct psychology may throw new light on old issues, a few topics have been selected for discussion.

Conformity

In the now famous Asch experiments (1951), groups were made up of one genuine subject and several 'stooges'. In a typical design, the group members were asked to state which of three lines on a card was equal in length to a line presented separately. In one of the trials in which the standard line was eight inches long, the majority exerted group pressure by saying that it was equal to the six-and-a-quarter inch line on the comparison card. As a result of this pressure, 37 per cent of the genuine subjects agreed with the majority.

Life does not often give us such invalidatory experiences and so what alternative does the poor person have available? In subsequent interviews most said they questioned their own judgement and not that of the majority before arriving at a decision. This seems reasonable for we seldom expect to be the only sane being in the midst of a group of mad people (except, seemingly, in a social psychology experiment). In the face of this overwhelming invalidating evidence, belief in our own judgement must be very strong indeed for us to hang on to it. Apparently, even those who had the courage of their convictions felt very uncomfortable, one reporting that 'despite everything, there was a lurking fear that in some way I did not understand I might be wrong — a fear of exposing myself as inferior in some way'.

Construing the events as 'well, I never was much good at measures anyway' was one way the subjects dealt with this invalidating evidence (a handy superordinate apparently more often used by women than men). Another reaction was to show Kellyian hostility. For instance, one subject convinced himself that he was sitting in a position which gave him a different visual angle to the lines from the rest of the group, which in turn gave him a distorted image. He was 'extorting validational evidence in favour of a type of social prediction which had already proved itself a failure'. If such experiments are to be conducted, it might well be more fruitful to make the focus of inquiry the reasons that led the subjects to respond in the ways they did, in terms of both their own construing and the different repertoire of reactions to invalidating evidence that construct theory proposes we all have available to us.

Among the most controversial of these 'deceiving' experiments has been the series by Milgram (1974). He appeared to show that quite ordinary people are willing to inflict severe pain in the form of electric shocks on subjects when they are told officially to do so by an experimenter in a laboratory experiment. Many variables affected the degree of painful shock the subjects were willing to inflict. For instance, the farther away the psychologist was the less obedient to instructions were the subjects. Some reduced the level of shocks when the experimenter was out of the room and lied about this when he returned. The nearer 'psychologically' subjects were to the victim, the less willing they were to participate. If they had to come close to or touch the victim, they were more likely to be disobedient. If the victim was in another room, it was apparently easier to inflict pain. And so on. The fact that this was play-acting on the victims' part (they were pretending to be writhing in agony at the shock, but no shock was actually received) does not alter the fact that these people thought they were inflicting pain and were prepared to do so *within a social experimental setting* and that variations in the social setting affected their willingness to participate.

Mixon (1972) looked at Milgram's experiments in some detail and argues that since the experimental situation is one that virtually demands compliance, it is strange that only 65 per cent of the subjects obeyed Milgram's orders instead of 100 per cent. By repeating the experiments using role-playing Mixon agreed that, from the onlookers' standpoint, this 65 per cent had performed an obviously immoral act. But he now saw that from their own viewpoint they had problems in construing the experimenter's construction process:

> From the outside the situation seemed clear, its definitions obvious. It was otherwise to the actors. They were not at all sure what was going on. The focus of much of their puzzlement was the behaviour of the experimenter. They could not understand why, when it looked as if something had gone seriously wrong with the experiment, the experimenter behaved as if nothing had happened. Far from being clear and obvious, the situation was mysterious and ambiguous. (Mixon, 1972, p. 78)

Mixon argues that subjects will conform in carrying out apparently inhumane acts provided they see no reason to believe that 'expected experimental safeguards have broken down'. In a situation in which the subject decides that the experimenter is ignoring evidence suggesting that something is seriously wrong, he or she will disobey.

Mixon advocated the use of the role-playing instead of deception as the basis of social research. But although the role-playing of such social situations may be an acceptable alternative to real-life laboratory situations, the morality of Milgram's experiments, in which subjects are deceived and sometimes disturbed, is clearly a rightful subject for discussion. In his experiments, the subjects were clearly put into what would, for many of us, be an emotionally disturbing situation, and some were indeed reported to be looking white and shaken when they had finished their work. Milgram says they were all told about the nature of the experiment afterwards and 'reassured', but how could he be sure that some were not permanently affected by having seen themselves as willing and able to inflict pain on others? One might argue that those subjects who were most distressed were those who had core constructs to do with 'making a good job of anything you take on' which was in conflict with the superordinate 'I am a humane person'. If the evidence confronting them was inconclusive, and their belief in the sanctity of holy experimentation profound, the subjects would be threatened in a very real way. They either had to risk doing a bad job by refusing to continue with the experiments or else risk being inhumane. A truly double bind. An interesting reflexive point is that Milgram himself seems to have felt that his position as scientist-experimenter justified him in trapping subjects into what can fairly be seen as a cruel situation.

Another approach to the study of conformity has been the attempt to identify the more as opposed to the less conforming person — that is, the trait of conformity. Bannister (1970b) has argued that trait theories are 'tautological in two senses — they inhibit the development of concepts of process and change and they produce unelaboratable concepts of original cause' (p. 412). In the case of conformity, it would advance our knowledge more if we were to study the type of interactive construing likely to produce agreement or nonagreement between people. If people construe themselves as being independent of others, set high store on forming their own opinions and do not believe that the majority usually knows best, then they are more likely to be nonconformist *in circumstances in which, for them, these constructs pertain*. If, on the other hand, they *either* stress the need to sum up each situation on its own merits *or* believe that one of the most valuable things in life is to get on with people, not upset them and so forth, then they will be more likely to go along with the ideas of others. Looking at individual construing systems in particular contexts will tell us more about agreement and disagreement than will measuring people on some scale designed to place each at some point along a 'conformity' continuum.

For instance, conforming behaviour in children has been investigated by Salmon (1969). But she did not seek some general characteristic of the child. Instead she investigated the extent to which the attitudes of the parents determined whether the child would be more likely to be influenced by other children or by adults. She concludes that:

> . . . the results also seem to support the view that conformity to particular social pressures is not an inborn characteristic of the subject, but is the outcome of his previous experience of crucial members of the relevant social groups. Boys who had experienced accepting rather than rejecting attitudes from their mothers tended to take *either* adults *or* peers as a reference group, rather than responding in an indiscriminate way to both. (Salmon, 1969, p. 30)

Prejudice

A potent source of social conflict and misery has been the resentment which minority groups of all kinds seem to arouse; in almost all cultures the 'out-group' is regarded with anxiety and hostility and treated as a threat. This reaction to others has frequently been termed 'prejudice'. A typical definition is that given by Krech, Crutchfield and Ballachey (1962): 'an unfavourable attitude towards an object which tends to be highly stereotyped, emotionally charged and not easily changed by contrary information'. If we review the kind of phenomena covered by the term 'prejudice' from a personal construct psychology standpoint, we can argue the immediate relevance of two major constructs from the theory.

Firstly, a 'prejudiced' argument involves an extensive use of constellatory and pre-emptive constructs. The constellatory construct which 'fixes the other realm membership of its elements' is characteristic of stereotyped or typological thinking — e.g. the view that if a man is black it necessarily follows that he must be *lazy, musical, highly sexed, low on washing* and *high on laughter*. But additionally and more dangerously, the prejudiced argument seems to use its constellatory constructs in a pre-emptive manner. The pre-emptive mode of using constructs is one which claims the elements of the construct for membership in its own realm *exclusively*. If this man is black he is *nothing but* a black; he is not simultaneously available to be viewed as a human being, a good gardener or a brother-in-law.

The second characteristic of prejudiced thinking arises from the linked notions of core constructs and hostility. It seems likely that for each of us our prejudiced ideas are core ideas, they involve dimensions along which we choose to see ourselves and others most significantly. Thus, any invalidation of our expectations in terms of these constructs would imply the need for a major revision of our outlook, a revision for which we may be ill-prepared. If these core ideas are experienced as being less meaningful, then we are threatened, we are made aware of 'imminent comprehensive change in our structures' (Kelly), or 'imminent comprehensive reduction of the total number of predictive implications of our personal construct system' (Hinkle, 1965). The disabled, for instance, may threaten us by demonstrating what is all too possible for ourselves.

Our reaction to such potential chaos is almost inevitably *hostility*. We refuse to be wrong, we set out to extort validational evidence for our prejudices, we cook the books, we deny the validity of sources of contradictory evidence. The essence of prejudice is that we use our constructs in a given area in an entirely non-propositional way; there are no 'ifs' or 'buts'. At best we might 'suspend elements' as in the classic statement 'some of my best friends are Jews'. 'Suspending elements' in this manner enables us to maintain our original prejudiced view. We hold these constructs to be major dimensions for making sense of central aspects of our life. Therefore, in order to safeguard our psychological stability or even our sanity we become hostile towards conflicting evidence.

To re-define such concepts as 'prejudice' in personal construct terms may look simply like playing the name-changing game. But it can be more than this. By talking in terms of constellatory constructs, core-role construing and so forth, we are bringing what was previously a relatively isolated area of study within a general framework so that it can be related to 'psychology' generally. It may be possible thereby to relate it to our construing of psychological change.

By definition prejudice is an attitude (constellation of constructs) which is resistant to change. We have argued that the resistance stems from the fact that the implications of the constellation of constructs are too extensive for the person lightly to undertake change — too much that is too personal is thereby entailed.

In the light of this argument consider, say, the study of Deutsch and Collins (1951) in which they were able to investigate change in degree of prejudice in a natural social experiment in America. They concentrated on two different types of housing estate — segregated and integrated. In the former there were different sections of the estate for blacks and whites, and in the latter allocation of houses was on the basis of the first come, first served — no note of colour being made against the name of the applicant. It was thus possible to study the reduction of prejudice, if any, as a function of the degree to which 'prejudiced people are brought into situations that compel contact between them and the objects of prejudice'.

These psychologists were arguing that such a situation would reduce prejudice providing that 'the intimacy and amount of contact with objects of prejudice not conforming to the stereotypes of the prejudiced are such as to result in experiences which are sufficiently compelling to resist marked perceptual and memorial distortion'. Leaving aside the mild air of tautology in this proviso, the experiment clearly showed that there had been a reduction in 'prejudice'. However, it also showed that the reduction was only a reduction and not complete elimination, and that for a number of people there had been no lessening in prejudice at all.

This suggests that simple experience *as such* is not an effective agent of change — it does not of itself guarantee reconstruction. Kelly repeatedly pointed out that we can have ten different experiences of an event if we reconstrue each time, or else have one experience *repeated* ten times if we fail to reconstrue. Prejudiced people, one suspects, are more familiar with the latter type of experience. It may be that the lessening of prejudice involves a change in the very way we construe, from constellatory and preemptive construing to propositional construing, largely without reference to particular objects of prejudice. By the strange economics of psychology it may be quicker and more effective to try to help people to recast their construing strategies altogether, as a method of lessening prejudice, rather than directly trying to persuade them that blacks, Jews, gypsies, homosexuals or Eskimos are really 'all right' people.

Additionally, we might note that such is the ingenuity of humans that we have ways of limiting the implications of our own stereotypes other than simply abandoning them. We can suspend elements from the range of conveniences of constellations of constructs — sometimes on such a scale that the constellation goes out of business. We find endless 'exceptions to the rule'. For instance, we can make ourselves exceptions to our own stereotypical rules even while accepting the 'truth' of the general statement. Stutterers hold the same stereotype of a 'stutterer' as do fluent speakers, yet make exceptions of themselves. They seem to be saying that others conform to this picture of the stutterer but 'I am different, I am unique, I stutter but I am not a stutterer' (Fransella, 1968, 1977). The same seems to occur with alcoholics (Hoy, 1973) and, nearer home, with men and women (Broverman *et al.*, 1972); that is, men's views of themselves differed significantly from their stereotype of 'men' and the same was true for women.

It has been suggested that constellatory or stereotyped construing helps us define ourselves as individuals. By knowing what a stutterer, alcoholic, man or woman *is* we can determine in what ways we are similar to, and yet different from, the stereotype; what is desirable for us and what is to be avoided (Fransella, 1977). Yet implicit in this is a problem. Stereotypes are not *only* constellations of constructs. The stereotyped description of a woman becomes a prescription of what a woman *ought* to be. Fransella and Frost (1977) end their book about women's perceptions of themselves by saying:

> Only if we move away from our stereotypes, can we change the world outside. And only in the process of changing the world outside can we begin to create new ways of seeing ourselves. The two cannot happen separately. (p. 205)

In our search for the ultimate psychological foundations and uses of prejudice we might look, not to sophisticated versions of the 'herd instinct' or to the notion of unfortunate reinforcement histories, but rather to our tendency to see our interpretations of the world as *facts* or reality out there, rather than simply as our interpretations of that reality. Only when we are enabled to see them as interpretations can we look for ways of changing both our interpretations and those 'facts'.

Change may come about because an existing 'simple' subsystem (e.g. prejudice) is proving to be inadequate for predicting the outcomes of our present behavioural experiments. We are aware of too many exceptions to our 'rules'. This may give rise to anxiety (the awareness that our existing system is unable to deal adequately with the events confronting us) and one response to this is aggression (the active elaboration of our perceptual field). Thus:

> Within limits, a person may be particularly aggressive in the area of his anxiety. This is the area in which his constructs seem partially to fail to embrace the events at hand within their proper ranges of convenience. In his effort to explore the uncharted area, the person may set up a rapid succession of choices and select alternatives among them. (Kelly, 1955, p. 509)

Howard (1970) argues that it is important to distinguish between hostility and aggression, from a construct theory viewpoint, when trying to understand the behaviour of others. As an example, he takes a problem met in management:

> When a man has placed a bet he cannot afford to lose on predictions which evidence keeps showing were quite invalid

and he keeps on extorting evidence or claiming the predictions occurred when it should be obvious that they did not, that man is hostile . . . When we find him in a position of considerable power in a firm, it is a serious matter both for him and that firm. His hostility tends to broaden its coverage and he becomes more and more incapable, despite frantic and clever efforts, of realistically validating some of his predictions. (Howard, 1970)

On the other hand, the aggressive man is one who has ideas and who is going places and who puts his ideas into practice whenever he can, no matter what the obstacles. He is often *called* hostile, but he is vastly different from the hostile man just described. One is as desirable in business as the other is destructive. Of course, this is equally as applicable in other walks of life, such as academia, where a life's work with a personally relevant theoretical system is put at risk by the increasing popularity and perceived significance of another system (Fransella, 1983).

Howard points out that it is all too easy to categorise people according to how their behaviour affects us — thus hostility and aggression are often seen as the same things because they are equally uncomfortable to live with. We are tempted to argue that a man *must* be hostile if his behaviour hurts us, workers *must* be motivated to strike because they hate the bosses or because they are being led by trouble-makers or because they are selfish. Perhaps if we used Kelly's first principle and went and asked the workers how they perceived their problems, we might be told. Told in the sense that we would be enabled to see *their* situation throught *their* eyes.

Communication and language

Surely a more impersonal approach to the study of communication in psychology than Leavitt's (1951) would be hard to find. Five people are allowed to communicate by posting messages through holes in screens. Solutions to simple problems are quickest if X can exchange information with all four others, but they cannot communicate with him. For complex problems, solutions are quickest if each can post messages to those on either side. Burgess (1968) has shown how some of the conflicting results obtained with this laboratory set-up were the inevitable outcome of the artificiality of the situation.

A personal construct approach would never lead one to embark on such mechanical experiments in the first place. Nor would it lead one to study group interaction by analysing the *quantity* of talk for each person. Borgatta and Bales (1953), for instance, analysed the amount of communication between members of groups who had not met before and classified them into high, medium and low communicators. Groups were then reconstructed so that they contained either all high, all low or all medium communicators plus a 'mixed' group. The highest rate of interaction and the highest satisfaction were in the mixed group.

But why stop there ? If we take this as a *starting point*, then we can try to isolate the reasons for the satisfactions. We can learn more about the satisfactions of different levels of communication for different people. What is it in the construing of one person that leads them to be silent whereas their partner talks vigorously? Micklem (1978) has made a start in this direction by looking at how silent and talkative sixth-formers construe themselves and are construed by others. The finding that the talkative boys saw themselves as being apart from the silent boys but the latter did not see themselves as set apart has clear implications for the future social well-being of this silent group.

If we literally speak the same language and use this as the basis of our attempts to communicate, it is all too easy to assume that the words used mean the same for each of us. While it is clear to the English that French is a foreign language, it is less readily accepted that the same verbal label may represent constructs that differ radically from person to person. For instance, when people speaking different languages have interpreters, how can the interpreter be sure that he or she is conveying the constructs that underlie the verbal labels? It is difficult enough when communicating directly.

It is when we are at our most ingenious and impressive that we present our fiercest challenge to traditional psychology. The artist, the humorist, the martyr, the mad person and the infant are virtually inexplicable in terms of conventional textbook psychology, and at a more everyday level the way we develop and use language is a mystery in its own right. Skinner's attempt to explain language on a learning theory basis in terms of simple associative connections collapsed in the face of Chomsky's simple point that there would not be enough time in a person's life for them to learn, word by word, the number of connections they obviously *know*. Clearly, we master *structure* (or more truly invent structure) and then use it freely to create infinite possibilities.

In contemplating language psychologists have followed their tradition of chopping the person into psychological pieces, and instead of creating theories of the person which would encompass language they have segmented language into an area of particular study — psycholinguistics. This has put us in the strange situation where theories of language and methods of studying language are developed separately from theories and methods which contemplate other aspects of behaviour — even 'cognition' has journals, institutes and methods of study largely disregarded by the separate devotees of language. This raises the issue of whether personal construct psychology can include 'language' within its range of convenience and encompass it within the same terms with which it discusses other aspects of the person.

Showing that this is indeed the case, du Preez (1972) analysed parliamentary debates of local South African affairs in 1948, 1958 and 1968 and compiled a dictionary of 120 constructs. By tracing the lines of implication for central constructs, he demonstrated that the parties construed reality in clearly different ways. Both then and more recently (1979, 1980), he has illustrated the way in which different ideological groups are talking different languages, with lines of implication from the main constructs which are logically irreconcilable. Thus, one party worked from the superordinate construct *survival of the white race*, another from *economic progress*, and the third from *humanitarian values*. The three groups were *psychologically* not talking to each other.

In another sense also we clearly do not have a language, we have languages. We seem to have a general, all-purpose, broad language for talking about ourselves and our world and in addition a large number of what might be called specialist or technical languages for talking about particular aspects of it — we have groups of terms (languages) for chemistry, chess, music, the internal combustion engine, economics and so forth.

These specialist languages seem to have their terms more closely defined — they seem to have gained in clarity of structure and implication by their constricted application. Agnew and Bannister (1973) sought to use the arguments of personal construct theory and facilities of grid method to examine whether the language of psychiatric diagnosis was one such specialist language or whether it was in fact 'pseudo-specialist'.

Diagnostic psychiatry claims the status of a technical language and is, indeed, constructed on the model of the specialist diagnostic language of general medicine. The characteristics of a specialist language, as distinct from lay language, can be argued to be that it has greater interjudge agreement between users as to how terms are defined and how they relate to each other. Specialist languages have greater stability over time, are less influenced by fashion and cultural change and are relatively uncontaminated by lay language. In this study eight consultant psychiatrists completed a series of four grids, each psychiatrist selecting 20 patients with whom they were familiar and about whom they had confidence in their judgement, to use as elements. At the beginning of the study each psychiatrist divided their patients randomly into two groups of ten and for one group rank ordered them in terms of eight *diagnostic* labels, that is, neurotic depression, personality disorder, schizophrenia, anxiety state, psychotic depression, hysteria, brain damage and obsessional neurosis. They then rank ordered their second group of patients in terms of eight *lay* psychological constructs, that is, generous, obstinate, considerate, reserved, unreliable, likeable, mature and submissive. Approximately one month later they repeated these grids, ranking their previously 'psychiatrically' judged patients in lay terms and *vice versa*. The relationship within the constructs of each language (in terms of rank order correlations) and the relationship between the languages was analysed for each psychiatrist.

The results showed that the degree of interjudge agreement about the relationship between constructs was no higher when the psychiatrists were using their professional psychiatric terms than it was when they were using ordinary lay terms. Note that what is under study here is not interjudge agreement in the sense of the different psychiatrists coming to the same conclusion about the same person (they each judged different patients). It is a more underlying kind of agreement or disagreement — do the *terms of judgement* (the constructs) relate to each other in the same way for different psychiatrists?

Secondly, it was shown that if the two sets of grids, completed one month apart, were compared then there was *equal* stability over time of construct relationships for the two languages.

Finally, it was shown that the two languages were in fact 'morally' contaminated with neurotic categorisation generally being seen as 'good' and psychotic characterisation being seen as 'bad'. Broadly, what was shown by the study was that diagnostic psychiatry is a *pseudo*-specialist system. It has the *style* of a well-defined and stable technical language which is agreed between professionals, but when its structure is examined it has all the ambiguities and imprecision of the ordinary language which we use to make psychological judgements about other people.

Apart from its particular implications for psychiatry, this study illustrates that language is within the range of convenience of the psychology of personal constructs. Likewise, Lemon (1975) has shown how language and construing interact in the bilingual, and Todd (1977) has explored religious belief, both as a commitment in life and as a language for describing that commitment. In somewhat different vein, Moss (1974) analysed the content and dramatic structure of *Hamlet* in terms of role construct theory. Methods generated by personal construct psychology can be used as tools for the exploration of those problems which are at present too rigidly copyrighted into the arbitrary domain of psycho-linguistics.

Social class attitudes

In a stratified society, each subgroup tends to have its own code of behaviour, manner of speaking and non-verbal forms of behaviour which serve to 'tell' strangers where each fits into the general social scene. Bernstein (1961) has suggested that in England there are also fundamental linguistic differences that influence how people psychologically organise their experiences; in other words, differences in how they construe. He follows Whorf (1956) in believing that the language we speak is an important determinant of how we think. Personal construct psychology contends that there is a close relationship between construing and language, but also that construing can be without verbal labelling as well. It cannot be reiterated too often that constructs are dichotomous discriminations, ways in which some things are experienced as similar and thereby different from others, and need not necessarily have verbal labels attached to them.

Bernstein (1959) stated that the middle and working classes in England speak virtually different languages, the former using an 'elaborated' linguistic code and the latter a 'restricted' one. Having described the characteristics of restricted speech, he goes on to say:

If some of the characteristics are examined — short, grammatically simple, syntactically poor sentence construction;

inappropriate verbal forms; simple and repetitive use of conjunctions; rigid and limited use of adjectives and adverbs; selection from a group of traditional phrases; the very means of communication do not permit, even discourage, individually differentiated cognitive and affective responses. (Bernstein, 1959)

He claims there is a vast difference in a mother calling to her child 'stop kicking that dog' and 'you must not be cruel to dumb animals'. Although Bernstein's ideas and research have been seriously criticised (e.g. Rosen, 1972), his general notions have relevance from our point of view. He is not talking so much about what would usually be called intelligence, but about a much wider issue; he is saying there is a whole way in which two groups may differ in how they organise their thought processes.

Warren (1966) put some of Bernstein's ideas to the test by giving forms of repertory grid to 30 sixth-form boys in a public school and to a group of day-release students at a technical college. They were selected so as to be homogeneous for social class within each group. He found that the middle-class boys related constructs in a more individualistic way, and comments that this was particularly striking since the public school boys were in fairly constant contact with each other, whereas the day-release boys met only once a week. One of the significant findings was unpredicted. The construct *unusual* was seen as something 'bad' by the working-class boys, whereas it was an independent construct dimension for the middle-class boys. Bannister (1962) had found that the construct *unusual* was also evaluatively 'bad' in the eyes of a group of patients diagnosed as neurotic. He argued that if neurotic individuals have simple, relatively inflexible, construct systems, then anything unusual would be seen as threatening and therefore undesirable. Warren concludes similarly:

. . . as a result of their restricted code the working-class group have less adequately organized cognitive systems, and will therefore tend to see any 'unusual' elements as something of a threat, since their construing systems are relatively less adequate for subsuming and predicting the behaviour of the 'unusual' element. (Warren, 1966, p. 262)

What remains to be done with this kind of study is to examine it reflexively to see how far it may be a case of middle-class researcher propounding middle-class values.

Cognitive complexity

Bieri (1966) has defined this as 'the tendency to construe social behaviour in a multidimensional way, such that a more cognitively complex individual has available a more versatile system for perceiving the behaviour of others than does a less cognitively complex person'. He argues that as a person develops socially so their ways of construing people become more complex; they have more ways or dimensions along which to perceive others.

Adams-Webber (1969) extended Bieri's ideas and method of analysis to investigate the notion that 'relatively cognitively complex persons will exhibit more skill than relatively cognitively simple persons in inferring the personal constructs of others in social situations'. To test this, he elicited constructs from 30 people, each person then showing how these related *for them* in a repertory grid. A person whose grid showed that they categorised people as, in general, having the same pattern of characteristics is relatively cognitively simple; a person who can visualise characteristics as being combined in a variety of ways is seen as cognitively complex. The cognitively simple person could be said to have a stereotyped view of people in seeing certain combinations of qualities as inevitably going together.

These subjects were called together again three weeks after completing the grids. They were grouped into pairs and told to imagine and discuss a holiday they would like to go on together, money being no object. When they had done this, they were each given a list of 44 bipolar constructs, 22 of which were those that had been elicited from their partner. It was these that they were required to identify. As Adams-Webber had predicted, the more cognitively complex the person, the more accurate they were in identifying which constructs had been elicited from their partner; perhaps because they were better able to take in other people's ideas compared with subjects who had only a few dimensions at their disposal with which to construe others.

Mueller (1974) further explored the area and found that cognitively simple people are more influenced by emotion when it comes to construing others than are those who are complex.

Canter (1970) related complexity to something other than person perception. Using a variation of the usual method of scoring

(McComisky *et al.*, 1969), he showed that architectural students who are complex in relation to construing buildings do much better in examinations than others who have fewer dimensions for such purposes. He also found that this was *not* related to intelligence as conventionally conceptualised and measured.

This example underlines the argument that describing construing as 'simple' or 'complex' is, at best, only meaningful in relation to specific construct subsystems. There is nothing to show that it can be used as a description of whole personal construct systems. There is need for much caution here. It would be very easy to fall into the error of thinking of cognitive simplicity-complexity as a trait dimension; as a scale along which a person earns a position and sits contented with all the glory ascribed to a datum. As Kelly said ' . . . an event seen only in terms of its placement on one dimension is scarcely more than a mere datum. And about all you can do with a datum is just let it sit on its own continuum' (1969c, p. 118). So let us not fall into the trait trap. Hall (1966) has shown that persons vary greatly in degree of complexity from subsystem to subsystem. That is, a person could well be extremely cognitively complex in relation to other people and yet simple when dealing with their family; or subtle when pondering paintings but crude on the topic of cats.

That this characteristic of construing can vary from situation to situation or from time to time does not mean it should not be studied. More information about the process will help us understand more about people and their reactions. Thus our suspicion that neurotics have relatively simple interpersonal subsystems leads us to try to help them elaborate this aspect of their construing, so enabling them to deal more readily with people's multiple quirks.

Person perception and interaction

Not all personal construct work in the field of person perception has been carried out purely in relation to cognitive structure. Bender (1968), for example, has found that if persons A and B are construed by C as being similar, then C considered that he or she would behave similarly towards them. Bender later (1976) extended this experiment and gained objective evidence that C actually did behave in the way anticipated.

Proctor (1985) has given us a theoretical account of the family dynamics in Kellyian terms and presented a grid method for examining the ways in which the members of a family interact.

An early experiment on how the perception of a person determines behaviour towards them was conducted by Kelley in 1950. Students were given identical descriptions of a visiting lecturer, except for one item: half were told he was 'very warm' and the others that he was 'rather cold'. After listening to the lecture, all rated him as intelligent but the 'warm' students rated him as more considerate of others, better informed, more sociable, more popular, better natured, more humorous and more human than did the 'cold' students. But these views also related to behaviour. During the succeeding discussion, 56 per cent of the 'warm' students participated actively whereas only 32 per cent of the 'cold' group did so.

The construct *warm-cold* is probably superordinate in most people's repertoire of personality constructs and thereby implies a multiplicity of subordinate ones. That differential construing of the lecturer led to differences in participation in communicating with him is a good illustration of the self-fulfilling prophecy ingredient in many of our acts of construing. We see X as 'cold', we treat X as 'cold' and then we truly find him 'cold'. Rathod (1983) has looked at other dimensions of interpersonal relationships.

How people are led to change their impression is the concern of Crockett and Meisel (1974). They used implications grids to obtain a measure of 'degree of connectedness' between subjects' constructs, and then set up a situation in which their predictions were validated or invalidated. In general, the more tightly connected the subjects' constructs, the more change occurred when their predictions met with strong invalidation. A change on one construct will mean changes on many others if all are relatively interknit. However, it was also found that where a core (self) or central construct was involved in the invalidation, there was little change. Clearly, here there was a threatening situation (awareness of imminent change in one's core construing) — *too many* important changes would be needed if our core construing has to be changed.

Duck has used a construct psychology approach to study the development of friendships (1973, 1979, 1983). He points out that Kelly provided the framework within which one can study person perception, impression formation and so forth, but provided little guidance about why, for instance, we like person A and dislike person B. Duck's theorising and research makes it seem that, in the first instance, we choose to establish a friendly relationship with another on the basis of similarity of the psychological descriptions we use of others (Duck and Spencer, 1972). The acquaintanceship starts on the basis of obvious similarity of attitudes, but Duck argues that similarity of attitudes is taken to imply similarity of construing at 'deeper' levels. When similarity is found to be at superficial levels only, then the friendship fails to develop. Duck goes on to argue (1979) that we set up a model of our friend, have expectancies concerning them and the relationship develops as these expectancies are validated or invalidated. Equally if not more important is the argument that the friend serves as validator of the hypotheses we have about ourselves. Personal construct psychology has clearly been fruitful here in stimulating both theoretical development and the experimental investigation of the hypotheses derived.

Directions

Kelly's suggestion that the notion of role could be a take-off point for a social psychology gives us not only new ways of tackling old problems but a way of unifying 'general' and 'social' psychology and abandoning the practice of seeing them as separate areas of study. That psychology must be stunted without integral concepts of 'sociality' is apparent. Leman (1970) suggested that if we wanted to try to answer the curious question 'where is the mind?', we might well say 'between people'. He was here stressing not simply our elaboration of ourselves through those we are directly involved with but our derivation from those who died long before we were born. The language we speak is our moulding of stuff we inherited — as are the constructs we use in our personal strategies; our mind is bequeathed to us, though we may give it a personal point and bequeath it as our own gift.

Thus little of significance is likely to come forth from those psychologists who study the 'isolated' functions of 'isolated' individuals. They cannot even draw a moral from the fact that their own style of experimental psychology was taught to them by a culture and they practise it as their continual interchange with that culture. But equally, without the construct of the individual person as the experiencing unit, social psychology becomes synonymous with sociology.

Speaking generally, the causation of insanity everywhere, special organic diseases apart, is an affair of the three w's — worry, want and wickedness. Its cure is a matter of three m's — method, meat and morality. (*Report of the Lancet Commission on Lunatic Asylums, 1875*)

For Kelly the focus of convenience of his personal construct psychology, however wide its range of convenience might be, was psychotherapy. It is not simply that he was a psychotherapist himself, but that he felt that people struggling with major personal issues would prove a scientifically more rewarding focus for psychology than the navigational problems of the rat.

Any attempt by one person to be of psychological help to another pivots on the relationship between the two people. Different formal approaches to psychotherapy seem to imply different kinds of relationship. The most traditional imply a 'doctor-patient' relationship which tends to encourage passivity in the allegedly ignorant patient while he or she waits for the ministrations of the expert doctor. A psychoanalytic approach to psychotherapy suggests a relationship more akin to that of priest and penitent, with absolution from the original sin of the Id as the ultimate goal. Some forms of client-centred psychotherapy adopt a stance which is reminiscent of that of an indulgent parent towards a child, while some cognitive therapists seem rather like authoritarian teachers in relation to their pupils. In behaviour therapy, the relationship seems to be broadly that of trainer-trainee. The relationship between psychotherapist and client envisaged by Kelly was essentially that of co-experimenters.

Before outlining a personal construct psychology approach to psychotherapy, one other approach — that of the behaviour therapists — will be discussed briefly for purposes of contrast.

Behavioural Psychotherapies

Behaviour therapy

Behaviour therapy (Wolpe, 1954) differs in many ways from most current methods for helping people with problems. It argues that 'symptoms' are learned maladaptive habits rather than the result of some underlying conflict. Since they are learned, they could be unlearned, for example, in the case of phobias, by substituting a relaxed feeling for one of fear or anxiety. Wolpe put it more formally:

> . . . when fundamental psychotherapeutic effects are obtained in neuroses — no matter by what therapist — these effects are nearly always really a consequence of the occurrence of re- ciprocal inhibition of neurotic anxiety, i.e. the complete or partial suppression of the anxiety responses as a consequence of the simultaneous evocation of other responses psychologically antagonistic to anxiety. . . (p. 205)

This reciprocal inhibition is sought by constructing hierarchies of feared situations ranging from one that produces virtually no fear to one that brings on sheer panic and then presenting these to the phobic person, a step at a time. They grow used to each situation either by being put into it, for example, by undertaking short excursions in the case of agoraphobics, or by being made to relax deeply and then to imagine the situation. Post Wolpe many variants of behaviour therapy (e.g. flooding, implosion and so forth) have been elaborated.

Kelly stated his view thus:

> Now what about 'behaviour therapy', which is supposed to be at odds with humanistic psychology, and precisely so because it is 'rigorously scientific'? To my mind the only thing wrong with the accounts of behaviour therapy I have read is that they fail to mention who the principal investigator was. They call him a 'subject', while the fellow with the doctoral degree, who turns out to be only the technician in the project, is given credit for doing the experiment . . .
>
> Take, for example, the reverse snake charming experiment, which has become the popular prototype for behaviour therapy. The task is for a person who shudders at the sight of snakes to

come to appreciate how very charming a snake can be. The first step is to entertain the hypothesis; although, like any proper hypothesis, it may not appear to be very realistic — at least not for the person engaged in the undertaking. The next step is to make a behavioural investment, that is to say, to pose the question behaviourally. That may not be what a philosopher would do, but it is what a scientist, who always doubts uncommitted rationality, must do. So the part to be played is the part of the scientist.

But a man making up to snakes may find himself floundering about in a multivariant predicament . . . one may find, in the presence of too many snakes, that his behaviour has lost its composed directionality. If the old boundaries of safety are to be transcended in his approach to snakes and there is to be a conclusion to the experiment, new boundaries must be established *ad hoc*. In research language this means that each successive experiment must be 'controlled' if the researcher is not to become lost in a sea of 'variables'. Moreover, the specific hypotheses in each sequential inquiry must be clearly defined, else the principal researcher will not be able to determine what is confirmed by what.

And there is one final ingredient in the science of being charmed by snakes. The scientist — I'm still talking about the fellow who is trying out a new slant on snakes — must be left free at the conclusion of each step to decide just what experiment is to come next. Here, as elsewhere, the outcomes of scientific endeavours are often best judged by what the scientist, after searching his own reactions to his completed undertakings, decides to do next. It is preposterous to assume that the mere overt outcomes of one experiment make the scientist's next venture a cut and dried affair.

Now let us notice how the Wolpe type of behaviour therapy artfully contrives a procedure to enable the patient to become his own experimenter. Preliminary interviewing focuses attention on the general hypothesis that he can learn to live with snakes. It is, of course, only a hypothesis and therefore a ventured departure from the reality of the patient's world. The criteria against which accurate predictions will be assessed are defined in terms of the state of relaxation the patient may experience. He then practises relaxation so he will recognize it when he sees it.

Next the patient's fear is calibrated and a useful scale of aversion is constructed out of a graduated series of pictures of snakes, or actual distances measured from the snake itself. Experimental controls are established as *ad hoc* boundaries which can be successively moved out as the patient becomes bolder. Fantasy, or make-believe, is employed as the patient imagines his approach to the snake before he actually attempts it . . . The patient is not pushed beyond the limits established for the current phase of his inquiry. Before each successive venture he must decide where the guard rails are to be placed, and he is free to return to their protective enclosure whenever he is threatened with incoherence. He does not surrender his in-itiative to another investigator. He observes carefully what happens — how frightened he is, or, rather, how relaxed he is, relaxation being operationally a better defined criterion for him than fright — and he notes how differently the snake appears as he approaches it. Finally, it is the patient, now a scientist planning his own actions, who decides what the next step in the experimental series will be. In this kind of therapy, behaviour is so clearly an experiment. (Kelly, 1970a, pp. 267-9)

Operant procedures

The use of systematic reinforcers to modify behaviour has been most widespread where more traditional procedures that lean heavily on verbal ability are not appropriate. Perhaps the most striking examples are those which came to be called 'token economy programmes'. Reinforcers are used to shape social behaviour such as the correct use of knives and forks, having trousers correctly zipped, making of beds. Whether with the long-stay adult psychiatric patient or the mentally handicapped child, the main problem here has been the lack of generalisation from the ward setting to the outside world.

The main problem with all these behavioural techniques is that they are very short on theory. Most have far outstripped learning theory which, in any case, was largely derived from animal experiments. A long-running debate in psychology is whether or not one can gener-alise from the animal to the human. A splendid example of where generalisation from animal to human was not valid is that given by Bijou and Bauer (1966) of the child whose responses were not extinguishing as required by the technique and, when asked why he continued to respond, said 'You didn't tell me to stop!'

The personal construct psychologist would not be surprised that such techniques do not generalise. The clients are coming to understand what the psychologists want of them *within a specific context*. They would have no reason to construe 'the outside world' as being the same as 'the ward'. To do this they would have to construe 'doing up my flies' as being something he, as an individual, saw as being meaningful *for him*. In theoretical terms this means developing some lines of implication from the specific behaviour at the subordinate level to a superordinate level of construing.

Cognitive therapies

Water Mischel credits Kelly with being the founder of cognitive psychology:

> Virtually every point of George Kelly's theorizing of the 1950's. . . proved to be a prophetic preface for the psychology of the 1970's and — it seems safe to predict now — for many years to come. Long before 'cognitive psychology' existed, Kelly created a truly cognitive theory of personality, a theory in which how people construe is at the core . . . There is reason to hope that the current moves toward a hyphenated cognitive-behavioral approach will help fill in the grand outlines that Kelly sketched years before anyone else even realized the need. (Mischel, 1980)

Personal construct therapy is often classed as a cognitive therapy. But it is not. It differs from the approaches of Beck (1976), Ellis and rational emotive therapy (Ellis and Grieger, 1977), or Meichenbaum (1977), by being based on an integrated, total psychological theory about the whole person and by giving primacy to neither cognitions nor emotions nor behaviours — there cannot be one without the others. In personal construct theory there is no dualism, no dividing up of the person into 'bits'.

Kelly was continually at pains to point out that cognitions were not of primary importance in his theory of the person. He once stated:

> In order to make the point, I have had to talk about constructs in such an explicit manner that I have probably given the impression that a construct is as highly articulate and cognitive

as my discussion has had to be. If I had been able to say what I said in metaphor or hyperbole I might have been able to convey the impression that a construct had something to do with formless urges too fluid to be pinned down by verbal labels. But personal construct theory is no more a cognitive theory than it is an affective or conative one. There are grounds for distinction that operate in one's life that seem to elude verbal expression. (Kelly, 1970), p. 15)

Since personal construct therapists have no problems with what causes what, they would not get involved in the current lively debate about primacy (e.g. Greenberg and Safran, 1984). A more detailed discussion of the relationship between personal construct psychotherapy and cognitive-behavioural therapy can be found in Neimeyer (1985; 1985a).

Personal Construct Psychotherapy

Approaches in psychotherapy all face the problem of defining 'what is wrong' with the client and thereby must select the terms in which 'wrongness' is to be specified. If we are *not* going to view the client as 'ill' or suffering from a 'maladaptive learned habit' or having 'failed to self-actualise' or as being 'tormented by Id-Super-ego imbalance', then what terms do we use? We can follow the scientist model through and see clients as people who are unable decisively to test out and elaborate their personal theories, their understanding of themselves and their interpersonal worlds. Their construing may have become circular, so that they are endlessly testing and retesting the same hypotheses and are unable to accept the implications of the data which they collect. They may have moved into the kind of chaos where constructions are so vague and loose that they cannot provide expectations clear enough to be tested and they simply flow back and forth around the same issues. Whatever the specific difficulty, the psychotherapist would never set out to sell a particular construct system to a client: they would seek to help the client to test the validity of the client's *own* construct system. If they are successful, in that the system once again begins to move and elaborate, then the direction in which it goes and the issues which it pursues are, in a very definite sense, no longer the psychotherapist's business.

Kelly outlined the therapist-client relationship thus:

We have ruled out the notion of psychotherapy as the confrontation of the client with stark reality, whether it is put to him in the form of dogma, natural science, or the surges of his own feelings. Instead, we see him approaching reality in the same ways that all of us have to approach it if we are to get anywhere. The methods range all the way from those of the artist to those of the scientist. Like them both and all the people in between, the client needs to assume that something can be created that is not already known or is not already there.

In this undertaking the fortunate client has a partner, the psychotherapist. But the psychotherapist does not know the final answer either — they face the problem together. Under the circumstances there is nothing for them to do except for both to inquire and both to risk occasional mistakes. So that it can be a genuinely cooperative effort, each must try to understand what the other is proposing and each must do what he can to help the other understand what he himself is ready to try next. They formulate their hypotheses jointly. They even experiment jointly and upon each other. Together they take stock of outcomes and revise their common hunches. Neither is the boss, nor are they merely well-bred neighbors who keep their distance from unpleasant affairs. It is, as far as they are able to make it so, a partnership.

The psychotherapy room is a protected laboratory where hypotheses can be formulated, test-tube sized experiments can be performed, field trials planned, and outcomes evaluated. Among other things, the interview can be regarded as itself an experiment in behavior. The client says things to see what will happen. So does the therapist. Then they ask themselves and each other if the outcomes confirmed their expectations.

Often a beginning therapist finds it helpful to close his cerebral dictionary and listen primarily to the subcortical sounds and themes that run through his client's talk. Stop wondering what the words literally mean. Try to recall, instead, what it is they sound like. Disregard content for the moment; attend to theme. Remember that a client can abruptly change content — thus throwing a literal-minded therapist completely off the scent — but he rarely changes the theme so easily. Or think of these vocal sounds, not as words, but as preverbal outcries, impulsive sound gestures, stylized oral grimaces, or hopelessly mumbled questions.

But at other times the therapist will bend every effort to help the client find a word, the precise word, for a newly emerged idea. Such an exact labeling of elusive thoughts is, at the proper time, crucial to making further inquiries and to the experimental testing of hypotheses. Particularly is this true when the team — client and therapist — is elaborating personal constructs. (Kelly, 1969d, pp. 228-30)

The theory can also be called upon to provide an explanation of why all of us resist change on occasion, whether or not in a psychotherapeutic relationship. For instance, the more implications, the more meaningful, or the higher the level of integration of the construct subsystem undergoing revision, the more difficult will be the change. Hinkle (1965) demonstrated this experimentally; Fransella (1972) found this in relation to improvement in those with stutters; Button (1980) replicated Fransella's findings with a group of those suffering from anorexia nervosa; and Sheehan (1983) found this dimension to relate to the amount of improvement found with a group of those being treated for depression. Resistance is also related to degree of anxiety, threat, superordinacy and several other variables (Fransella, 1985).

Looked at from the standpoint of personal construct psychology, many current psychotherapies are better viewed as *techniques* rather than as total approaches in their own right. Thus a personal construct psychotherapy might well include behaviour therapy methods if, for instance, the client was having difficulty in tightening construing in a given area. It might include a psychoanalytic type of free association if the patient had difficulty in loosening constructs. But the personal construct psychotherapist would retain throughout the view that clients are essentially experimental scientists in their own right, rather than people to be manipulated by the behaviour therapist or absolved by the analyst. For more detailed accounts see Bannister (1975); Epting (1984); Landfield and Leitner (1980); Fransella (1985a); and Button (1985).

Fixed Role Therapy

As one particular technique to be used with some clients, Kelly formulated the idea of fixed role therapy. It is in no way a panacea — rather it is a moderately useful technique when the psychotherapy has become circular and some trigger for movement is required. But it embodies and illustrates many of the ideals of construct theory psychotherapy.

The therapist first asks the client to write a self-characterisation. The client writes in the third person (beginning, say, 'Sue Brown is . . .') from the viewpoint of a sympathetic friend. The psychotherapist examines this self-portrait and (usually in collaboration with another psychologist) draws up a fixed role sketch which is a portrait of a person who is psychologically at 90 degrees to the self-characterisation of the client. The client is going to be asked to play the person described in this fixed role sketch and should not be presented with a portrait of someone who is their diametric opposite. It is difficult and threatening to enact an exactly opposite person and, in any case, the primary problem in development is to find new dimensions along which to see one's life, not to slot-rattle to the other end of dimensions which are already far too fixed. Thus, the fixed role sketch is something that would involve the client in new but not over-demanding ventures; for example, if they see their relationships as concerning *dominant* versus *submissive* then the fixed role sketch might describe a person who is fiercely *interested* in people but not, thereby, either dominant *or* submissive.

This fixed role sketch is shown to the client and they are asked if they find such a person credible. If they do not, the fixed role sketch is altered until they do. Next they are asked if they would find such a person broadly likeable. If they do not, the fixed role sketch is altered until they do. The client is then told that for a brief period (say three weeks) they are to be the person in the fixed role sketch. The client is to eat the kind of food they think this person would eat, read the books they would read, respond to other people in the way in which this person would respond, dream the dreams this person would dream, and try to interpret their experiences entirely in terms of this 'person'. It should be made clear to the client that this is a limited venture and that after a fixed period it will come to an end and they will revert 'to being themselves'. It must be made clear that the fixed role is in no sense being set up as an ideal, it is merely a hypothesis for them to experiment with, a possibility for them to experience. During the short period of fixed role enactment the client sees the therapist frequently to discuss the interpretation of the fixed role, to consider the kind of experiences they are getting and to play the role with the therapist.

At the end of the fixed role enactment it is hoped that the client will have experienced behaviours from people of a kind not likely to have been elicited by their usual 'self'. They will have been forced into a detailed psychological examination of this imaginary person and thereby have been less centred on themselves. Above all, they may have begun to suspect that a person is self-inventing and that they are not necessarily trapped forever inside their own autobiography and their own customary thought and behaviour.

Details of the technique of fixed role therapy are available in Kelly (1955), Bonarius (1970), Karst and Trexler (1970), Skene (1973) and Epting (1984). The point of stressing it in this context is to illustrate the emphasis on personal exploration and experiment which is the essence of construct theory psychotherapy. However, it must be remembered that Kelly described the method only as an example of how a therapist *might* work with *some* clients within a framework of personal construct psychology.

Personal Reconstruction

Since we see processes psychologically channellized by one's construction system, we can view them as being changed, either by re-routing through the same system of dichotomous constructs, or by reconstruction of the system of channels. In the clinic one is more apt to be concerned with the latter kind of readjustment. The former type is sometimes referred to as the 'Dean's Office treatment'. It could also be called, quite appropriately, 'lawyer treatment'. But the latter kind of readjustment is a much more ambitious undertaking and involves many technical difficulties, both in communication and in timing. Yet we see it as the ultimate objective of the clinical-psychology enterprise, and have used it as the basis for the theme of this book — *the psychological reconstruction of life*. We even considered using the term *reconstruction* instead of *therapy*. If it had not been such a mouth-filling word we

might have gone ahead with the idea. Perhaps later we may!
(Kelly, 1955, p. 187)

The stutterer

An example of the application of the theory to explain a
phenomenon and on the basis of this to plan a programme of
'treatment' or reconstruction is work on stuttering (Fransella,
1972; Meshoulam, 1978). A person is, psychologically, nothing but
a bundle of constructs, or so says Kelly (being pre-emptive for
emphasis). This being the case, then people must stutter because
they view their world in some particular way. Stuttering could, of
course, be viewed as a neurological abnormality, an anatomical
defect or a personality disorder, but in a review of the literature
(Beech and Fransella, 1968) the conclusion was reached that there
was little evidence to suggest that any of these ways of viewing
stuttering profited us much. And the situation has not changed
since then. In any case let the neurologists look for neurological
defects, anatomists or surgeons for anatomical defects and
psychologists construe in psychological terms.

A person's aim, according to personal construct psychology, is
to make the world as meaningful a place as possible. The more
meaningful one way of behaving becomes as opposed to its
alternatives, the more difficult it will be to change that behaviour.
One can think of the lifelong stutterer as being a person who has
built up a very elaborate subsystem of constructs to do with being a
'stutterer' and only sketchily construes being a 'fluent
speaker' — they have indeed had little opportunity of experimenting as a fluent speaker. They therefore cannot readily
change from stuttering to fluency — no one voluntarily walks the
plank into the unknown depths of the ocean. Would there not be
conceptual chaos if you were told that tomorrow you had to go out
into the world as a member of the opposite sex? Your behaviour to
men and women might have to be radically changed; how many
gestures, mannerisms, ways of talking or walking or sitting would
be misconstrued? Such a radical change would arouse extreme
anxiety in the majority of people because of '*the awareness of the
relative absence of implications with respect to the constructs with
which one is confronted*'. Imagine also the threat in that situation
because of '*the awareness of an imminent comprehensive reduction
of the total number of predictive implications of the personal construct system*' (Hinkle, 1965).

Here, then, is a personal construct theory explanation of stuttering — that a person stutters because it is from this stance that the world is most meaningful to them. Before they can become a fluent person, this 'state of fluency' would have to be made more meaningful to them.

In a study of 20 stutterers (Fransella, 1972), this was achieved by concentrating on the construing of fluency. The vast majority of stutterers, no matter how severe their disability, have moments of fluency. It was these that formed the basis of construct change and elaboration. Each fluent episode was discussed in great detail — *the stutterer was made to construe it*, everything about it. Only too often one finds that the stutterer has not done this when fluent. They have construed it globally as 'I was not stuttering'. They have not looked to see what difference this made to how they felt and behaved, how the listener reacted and what aspects of the situation might have led to their being fluent. The focus is on the *joint* search for common denominators in such situations.

To guide the self-exploration process and to give some quantitative data for comparison with changes in disfluencies, Impgrids were used. To monitor the relative meaningfulness of being a stutterer as opposed to being a fluent speaker, two such grids were repeated over time for each stutterer. For the 'stutterer' (S) grids, constructs were elicited by presenting triads consisting of two photographs of people and a card on which was written *the sort of person people see me as being when I am stuttering*. The same procedure was followed for the 'non-stutterer' (NS) grids, except that the card read *the sort of person people see me as being when I am NOT stuttering*. These elicited constructs were then laddered (see Chapter 3, p. 50). By termination of treatment 13 out of 17 had reduced their disfluencies by more than half, seven of these by more than 80 per cent.

Each stutterer also wrote a self-characterisation at the time of doing the Impgrids and having speech recordings made. These often gave quite different information from that elicited by the triadic method. In this case it may partly have been because the constructs elicited for the Impgrids were concerned with the stutterers' views of themselves in speaking situations, while the self-characterisations were concerned with their global construing of themselves *as persons*. Examples of the change that can be brought about in a person's view of the world can be seen in the following extracts from two self-characterisations by the same person.

At start of treatment programme

X is basically a worrier, which produces the attitude that things that go too well can't last. He is a serious person who was rather shy and something of an introvert in his youth. Today, however, he has removed many evils of those attitudes. He worries constantly about the impression he gives other people and tries to please and be popular in all forms of social intercourse. He has a very warm and human personality and although he regrets not having had a good education he has, through his own efforts largely, educated himself. His stammer has prevented him from allowing his personality to develop to the full as a non-stammerer's would be able to, and he feels unequal in an unequal world.

Lastly, his happily married life has given him a necessary sense of responsibility for his family, from which stems the respect and love he seeks.

Eighteen months later

Today, X is a confident, self-sufficient person who through his own strong determination plus sympathetic external help has become a useful member of society.

He is now perfectly capable of taking his place in this tough competitive world. He is now leading a busy, active life and his lifelong stammer that has dogged him has been largely overcome.

People who meet him for the first time would find him mildly aggressive but always prepared to be interested in others' problems. Lastly, he will not suffer fools gladly.

Interestingly, X begins by seeing himself at the *shy* end of a *shy-sociable* dimension. He concludes by not seeing himself at the *sociable* pole of construct but by seeing himself at the *aggressive* end of a new *aggressive-submissive* dimension. Note also that he views the change as largely his own achievement.

One unpredicted finding of the study was that as the non-stutterer system became more meaningful so the other *undiscussed* stutterer system became less so. As one set of constructs is elaborated and validated so the other set is invalidated. We might wonder how far disuse is the functional equivalent of invalidation.

It may be that this concentration on the *construing* of fluency situations is the common denominator in successfully treated clients. Stutterers improve and remain improved if they are able to take advantage of instances of fluency by actively construing them. Others have the same fluent episodes but do not *experience* fluency.

A factor of prognostic significance was than those who had more implications to do with being a stutterer at the start of therapy (it was the more meaningful to them) were less likely to become fluent than those whose subsystem of constructs to do with stuttering was less tightly-knit.

A further study has been conducted comparing a behaviour modification approach on its own and when combined with a personal construct approach. From Fransella's earlier study it was predicted that those who were helped to construe their new-found fluency would have lower rates of relapse than the behaviour modification group. This was, in fact, found to be the case (Evesham and Fransella, 1985).

This same theoretical approach has been applied to the treatment of other long-standing problems such as obesity (Fransella, 1985b), anorexia nervosa (Fransella and Button, 1984) and phobias (O'Sullivan, 1985). It is equally applicable to gambling and smoking. People are unlikely to 'give up' something that is an integral part of themselves unless they become aware of the personal implications of the alternative (desired) behaviour.

The depressed person

Rowe (1978, 1983) has given a novel slant to the understanding of depression. She takes the personal construct stance in seeing a person's problems as only understandable if we can see events and people as that person sees them. It is less helpful to try to understand them according to the clustering of 'symptoms' which give rise to a diagnosis of 'depression'. She argues that each child builds up a system of constructs as it interacts with other people. Part of this system is concerned with how we prevent too much interaction. We may place inhibitions on interaction under the rubric of 'I keep myself to myself'. These constructs are like bricks in a wall which we build around ourselves:

Some people build low walls, or walls with special gaps, and they can reach others easily across these walls. But some of us build walls which are high and difficult to climb, and when we make these walls too high, quite impassable, then we start to suffer a torture which is even worse than that suffered by the solitary prisoner facing an indeterminate sentence. (Rowe, 1978, p. 30)

Like Fransella, Rowe sees change as only being possible when we have some understanding of where we are going — if there is only chaos out there, we will not move. Rowe's psychotherapy focuses on trying to understand the metaphors and myths that are an integral part of any personal language system (cf. Mair, 1977a). For instance, Rowe describes how cleanliness for Rose was of vital importance. She needed rest but was unable to take it. During the course of psychotherapy it transpired that it was only possible to face the Day of Judgement if you help others and are clean. Since one never knows when that Day is coming, it is important always to be ready:

I've scrubbed every bit of that pantry and I've got my door painted white and I've done all my windows which wanted doing and I'm quite satisfied now. I get my Hoover out and I do the passage out and the bedroom and downstairs and every time I have a bath I wash it straight out. I keep my windows clean. I keep my clothes clean. I keep myself clean, every night I have a bath, so I know if anything happened I'm clean. (Rowe, 1978, p. 128)

Would *you* be able to rest if you were Rose?

Others have also found personal construct theory a useful framework from which to explore and understand depression. Jones (1985) has focused on its creative aspects; Sheehan (1983) has studied the aspects of reconstruction that accompany the lifting of depression; Neimeyer has also looked at reconstruing during therapy for depression with individuals (1985b), within a group context (Neimeyer, Heath and Strauss, 1985), and from a personal construct theoretical perspective, (Neimeyer, 1984).

But the principles outlined for the stutterer and the depressed person who choose to change are not only relevant to those wishing to embark on such radical experiments. We all choose to change many times during the course of our lives. We often say that it is our circumstances that have changed, as when we seek to become married rather than single, or a farmer rather than a clerk.

Radley (1974) visualised such changes proceeding much as those outlined for the stutterer. The change from labourer to foreman could be a three-stage process. Firstly, we have to be able to visualise what it is to be a foreman. Radley is arguing that, just as for the stutterer, we need something quite tangible in the way of a picture of the future state to aim at. We need to be able to fantasise it in some detail, to construe it, to anticipate what it will be like in vivid terms. If our vision of what it is to become a 'foreman' is murky, then we will not actively engage ourselves in the attempt, however attractive the idea might be 'in theory'. We will not choose to move towards something we cannot sense. In the second stage we begin to enact our goal, we behave as if we were foremen. Note that Radley is here talking about the psychology of change. We may well by now have become 'fore-men' in the eyes of the world and in terms of the label on our pay-packet, but we may not yet have become 'foremen' within ourselves. In the third stage the enactment becomes the truth, it is truer of us to say that we are, in the way we walk and talk and construe, 'foremen' than to say we are 'labourers'.

As a good personal construct psychologist, Radley (1978) moved on, in his essay 'The opposing self', to discuss the contrast pole — the process of hindered change. In like manner, one can study what hinders the stutterer in taking the route to fluency. Cochran (1976) has experimentally elaborated our understanding of how we may change our construct systems when faced with puzzling information. In doing this he is extending work which dates as far back as the pioneer paper of Levy (1956).

Measurement and Understanding the Complaint

Bannister and Bott (1973) conducted a series of treatment studies in which both the evaluation and understanding of the complaint and statements of hoped-for change were examined in grid terms. Grid results guided the course of treatment. The following is a characteristic case.

Following an industrial accident which left him a semi-cripple with an artificial leg, the patient became severely depressed, subject to outbursts of intense anger, suffered from headaches, was tense, uninterested in his leisure and unable to contemplate further work. Psychotherapy focused on the problem of helping the patient to adjust to the idea of himself as 'a man with an artificial leg'. The aim was to help the patient recover from what he and the therapist thought of as the psychological consequences of the accident. For a longish period psychotherapy was markedly unsuccessful and eventually the patient was given a grid in an attempt to facilitate a better understanding of the way in which he saw himself and other people.

In this grid, the patient made judgements about ten people who were important in his life — his wife, a close friend, a person towards whom he had always been antagonistic and so on. The names of people were presented to him in threes, and he was asked to indicate some important way in which two of them were alike and thereby different from the third. For one triad, he said: these two *have confidence in themselves*, the third *has no confidence*. This, therefore, is presumably one way in which he sees people as different from each other; it is one of the 'personality dimensions' he considers important. In this way, 14 constructs (two poles for each construct) were elicited and three *(like me, like I'd like to be* and *like I used to be)* were supplied by the psychologist.

On each construct-dimension, the patient rank-ordered his ten people — from, say, the *most confident* down to the *least confident*. The completed grid was analysed by working out the correlations between each rank-ordering. For example, the patient tended to rank as high on *like I am* those people ranked low on *understanding*. There was a negative correlation of -0.76 between the two constructs. This can be taken to imply that, in grid terms, he does not 'see' himself as an understanding person.

One cluster could be described as comprising *my moral ideal* versus *opposite to my moral ideal*, judging by the way constructs related to it. The second cluster was difficult to describe — it could be labelled *my practical ideal*. Note that, in thus labelling the clusters, we are following traditional practice and trying to summarise the mathematical relationships *in our own terms*. We should beware of becoming too attached to any such imposed labelling — it is psychological guesswork.

This patient had presented himself in interview as a once happy and well man who now had problems all caused by an accident which had left him a cripple with an artificial leg. Yet the position of *like I used to be* in the grid suggests a long-standing discrepancy between his picture of himself and his ideals (*like I would like to be*). Moreover, although he argued that a loss of working efficiency was the essence of his problem, his ideal was more closely related to interpersonal constructs such as *understanding, good mixer* and *trusting*.

Following the implications of this grid, the focus of the psychotherapy was changed. Patient and therapist began to explore the patient's relationships with other people as they had evolved throughout his lifetime. The question of work was left temporarily unanswered and the issue of 'being a man with an artificial leg' was left entirely on one side. It was assumed that however traumatic the industrial accident may have been, the problems at issue long pre-dated it and must be discussed as if they were, in some ways, independent of it. This approach was successful in that he elaborated his interpersonal relationships *and* adapted to the artificial leg and to new work.

It is important to bear in mind here that the argument is not that this way of formulating the problem was true and the earlier formulation was false, nor to deny that there were probably several other ways of viewing the problem which might have been more or less helpful. The essential lesson is that the formulation and reformulation of the problem, the different ways in which questions can be asked, are an *integral* part of the psychotherapeutic process itself, not an issue settled irrevocably by 'correct' diagnosis before therapy begins. Surprisingly often in successful psychotherapy the problem initially presented by the client is bypassed and much broader life issues become the focus.

The lesson presumably applies to our ways of formulating problems in our personal lives. Those who are still prone to think in terms of a 'real illness' *or* 'real symptom' *or* 'real Oedipal conflict' model should remember the science fiction story about a homicidal maniac who buys a home psychotherapy machine to cure him of killing. The salesman sells him, in error, a Martian model which succeeds in 'curing' him of a Martian psychosis called 'feem desire', after convincing him that he has got it.

Ryle and Lunghi (1969) have suggested that such a construct analysis approach should be used in the evaluation of the outcome of psychotherapy. Most studies of the effects of psychotherapy rest on socially defined and generalised measures of improvement. No one ought arbitrarily and generally to decide what is the criterion of improvement. Ryle suggests that the desired effects of any treatment should be stated beforehand *for each client*. Kelly (1980) spells out some of the criteria a personal construct therapist might use in 'A psychology of the optimal man'.

Change in relationships

Another approach to the study of outcome focuses on the degree of closeness of the complainer's and helper's use of certain constructs. Cartwright and Lerner (1963) found that patients having client-centred Rogerian therapy were more likely to improve if the therapist increased his or her 'understanding' of them during treatment. Understanding or empathy was measured by the similarity between the client's construing of themselves (using ten elicited constructs) and the therapist's use of these constructs in role-playing the client. Additionally, clients were more likely to improve if they saw a 'need to change', this being the difference between how they saw themselves at the start of treatment and how they hoped to be at the end. Landfield (1971) found, using grids, that therapists who used their clients' construing language were less likely to have them opt out of treatment.

Bannister and Bott (1973) have studied the interpersonal perception between husband and wife as a basis for marriage counselling. They elicited constructs from both partners and asked them to use these independently in a form of rank-order grid. Both sets of constructs were then combined into one grid and the couple completed this second grid *together*, giving their agreed judgements. This procedure of obtaining two independent grids and a joint (duo) grid was repeated several times throughout counselling; the separate grids were correlated with the 'duo' grid to show who was the dominant partner. Dominance (the higher correlation between individual and duo grid) proved to be related to the absence or presence of any sexual contact (the primary problem). When the husband was dominant, sexual contact was minimal and when the wife was dominant, as on the second testing occasion, increasing sexual contact was noted.

This work suggests a possible change in psychologists' notion of 'group' tests. Traditionally, group tests are simply standard tests applied individually to each member of a group. Much might be explored by letting groups complete a single test by arguing out and agreeing a group response, thereby showing something of the consensus and interplay of the group.

The importance of considering relationships in the context of change has been emphasised by Ryle and Lunghi (1970). They comment that constructs elicited from people attending for psychiatric help most often relate to interpersonal behaviour, but are then applied to elements in general. They give the example 'in rating John on the construct *is understanding*, the rater must make an overall judgement which might take no account of John's relative lack of understanding of Jill, or of his exceptional under- standing of Elizabeth'. They therefore developed a 'dyad trid' in which the elements are relationships and not individuals (e.g. John in relation to Jill, John in relation to Elizabeth and so forth). This dyad grid has been found useful in aiding understanding of marital problems and has been used with a 'reconstruction' grid designed to measure change (Ryle and Lipshitz, 1975).

Change in the group

Personal problems are often seen as a breakdown in social rela- tionships and so it seems logical that these problems should be sorted out in a social setting. Group psychotherapy has evolved largely to provide such a social setting. Kelly described the stages through which a psychotherapy group could be guided to enable each member ultimately to achieve independence of group support. These stages include acceptance or 'readiness to see the world through another person's eyes', group role-playing centred on relationships within the group, the enactment of situations outside the group and finally experimenting with roles outside the group.

Early studies which reported on the use of theory and grid method in the exploration of group processes included those of Fransella and Joyston-Bechal (1971), Fransella (1970) and Watson (1970). These investigators all used the members of the group as elements; that is, each member of the group rated or ranked themselves along with others in the group in terms of certain constructs. In each case the verbal labels were supplied by the investigators. Although this supplying of adjectives is not desirable if the aim is to get to know the specific constructs of individual group members, in practice it is extremely difficult to make con- tent comparisons across group members without standardising the verbal labels. (It should be remembered that the *construct- discriminations* are not supplied, only words which the subjects interpret in terms of their own constructs.)

Interesting things happen when change in process as well as content is looked at during the psychotherapeutic period. Changes along the 'tight-loose' dimension can occur among the majority of members. Not only this, but the changes happen broadly *at the same time*. Further, they are not limited to those actively participating in the discussions, but include the psychotherapist as well as the person who sits silently present in order to make an 'objective' assessment of what has occurred (Fransella and Joyston-Bechal, 1971). That some such fluctuation occurs is not a new idea (e.g. Rogers, 1958: Walker *et al.*, 1960; Argyris, 1969), but construct theory enables hypotheses concerning its occurrence to be made and possible causal relationships to be investigated. Argyris (1969) has commented that successful T-groups move from 'tight' to 'loose' construing during the course of their meetings. Perhaps by looking at this through construct theory goggles we can hope to find out why they are successful.

Another measure in the Fransella and Joyston-Bechal study assessed the extent to which each person was able to perceive how the other members saw them. For most of the group, people who saw themselves as being *like the therapist* were so seen by the group. On the other hand, they were most inaccurate in perceiving, or admitting to perceiving, that they were *disliked*. The only two people rated as showing significant therapeutic improvement were the two who were *most* accurate in seeing how others saw them in terms of the constructs used in the gird. They were also the people who had no significant fluctuation over time in their tightness of construing.

There was a tendency for the psychiatrist to see 'tight' construing as contra-indicating improvement. Most theoretical positions support this view, but it was surprising that the psychiatrist considered *accuracy* of perceiving how others saw them as also contra-indicating improvement. The picture gets even more cloudy when we consider that the only two people who were judged by *independent judges* to have improved were the two who did not vary on the 'tight-loose' dimension and who were most *accurate* in perceiving how others saw them.

One of the limitations of supplying constructs in psychotherapy research is that one is unable to study the therapist's construing of the group. However, McPherson and Walton (1970) did elicit constructs from clinicians who had observed at least 25 meetings of a single psychotherapy group. Each did a grid and these were combined into a single grid which was analysed into its principal components (Slater, 1976). The first component was *dominance-*

submissiveness; the second *emotionally sensitive to others-emotionally insensitive to others* and the third *hinders attainment of group goals-aids attainment of group goals*. The second component contains constructs such as *ability to feel with others-involved only with self; sensitive to others' feelings-insensitive to others' feelings*.

A later study by Caplan and colleagues (1974) has shown how feelings of self-esteem and early patterns of family relationships (as revealed by grid method) correlate with the verbal behaviour of people in a group — speaking, being spoken to and kinds of topic introduced. Fielding (1975) has demonstrated the grid's usefulness as a device for measuring outcome in diverse types of psychotherapy group, while Morris (1977a) examined, among other issues, the way in which the personal problems of the psychotherapy group leaders fared in the course of the group's life.

Studies such as these support the contention that construct theory and grid technique may shed light, not only on individual problems, but also on processes underlying group interaction.

Kelly saw the purpose of psychotherapy as liberation — it should enable the clients to escape from the imprisoning contradictions of their own view of life. He summarised kinds of personal re-invention in psychotherapy as follows:

> The team of client and therapist can go about their task in a variety of ways. Essentially these are the same ways that, on one kind of occasion or another, man has always employed for dealing with perplexities. (1) The two of them can decide that the client should reserve his position with respect to one of the more obvious reference axes. Call this slot rattling, if you please. It has its place. (2) Or they can select another construct from the client's ready repertory and apply it to matters at hand. This, also, is a rather straightforward approach. Usually the client has already tried it. (3) They can make more explicit those pre-verbal constructs by which all of us order our lives in considerable degree. Some think of this as dredging the unconscious. The figure is one that a few have found useful; but I would prefer not to use it. (4) They can elaborate the construct system to test it for internal consistency. (5) They can test constructs for their predictive validity. (6) They can increase the range of convenience of certain constructs, that is, apply them more generally. They can also decrease the range of convenience and thus reduce a construct to a kind of

obsolescence. (7) They can alter the meaning of certain constructs; rotate the reference axes. (8) They can erect new reference axes. This is the most ambitious undertaking of all.
(Kelly, 1969d, p. 231)

The techniques used for achieving these kinds of change can range
through behavioural exercises, free association, role-playing and
many not yet invented. This must not be confused with
eclecticism. The unchanging theme of the approach is the use of
theoretical constructs about the process of change and the
partnership it prescribes for 'therapist' and 'client'. These are
abstract enough to subsume the diverse multitude of personal
concerns which people in therapy will present and reasonably hope
to have understood.

THE PERSON AS SELF-CREATOR
AND SELF-DESTROYER

> If we are to have a psychology of man's experiences, we must
> anchor our basic concepts in that personal experience, not in
> the experiences he causes others to have or which he appears to
> seek to cause others to have. (Kelly, 1969e)

Traditional psychiatry has encouraged us to cling to the notion of
'mental illness'. It has formalised this into diagnostic categories so
that we are not deeply unhappy, we suffer from a 'depressive
illness', we are not gravely confused, we suffer from
'schizophrenia', and so forth (Bannister, 1985).

But if we think of people not as belonging to illness categories
but as individuals who have problems, we are irrevocably led to
the position of asking people what their trouble is. We can then try
to understand their way of viewing the world so that we can help
them to work out an alternative way of relating to others and to
their environment.

An example of this 'introspective' (Rychlak, 1968) attempt to
deal with personal problems is given by Wright (1970). In his
paper 'Exploring the uniqueness of common complaints', he says:

> A symptom may be regarded as a part of a person's experience
> of himself which he has singled out and circumscribed as in
> some way incongruous with the rest of his experience of
> himself. It is normally something experienced as issuing from
> his *person*, but incongruous with his *view of himself* ('his self').
> On account of the incongruity with the 'self', it tends to be
> regarded as *non-self* and is offered by the person as that which
> requires treatment (removal) . . . (Wright, 1970, p. 222)

Wright goes on to say that there are two approaches the therapist
can take to the sufferer: he or she can fix them into some 'illness'

or maladaptive response framework or can explore with them what it is in their construing that has led to the present impasse. The former approach exploits the person's conviction that part of their behaviour is alien to them by encapsulating the problem in the medical model. Wright's study offers an excellent account of how a particular person reconstrued her 'symptoms'.

Personal construct theory differs from personality theories centred on the 'self' in that the self is seen as a construct along with all other constructs, albeit a very important one. Kelly introduces the idea of self as follows:

> Let us turn our attention, more particularly, to the controlling effect one's constructs have upon himself. As we have pointed out before, the *self* is, considered in the appropriate context, a proper concept or construct. It refers to a group of events which are alike in a certain way and, in that same way, necessarily different from other events. The way in which the events are alike is the self. That also makes the self an individual, differentiated from other individuals. The self, having been thus conceptualized, can now be used as a thing, a datum, or an item in the context of a superordinate construct . . .
>
> When the person begins to use himself as a datum in forming constructs, exciting things begin to happen. He finds that the constructs he forms operate as rigorous controls upon his behavior. His behavior in relation to other people is particularly affected. Perhaps it would be better to say that his behavior *in comparison* with other people is particularly affected. It is, of course, the comparison *he* sees or construes which affects his behavior. Thus, much of his social life is controlled by the comparisons he has come to see between himself and others. (Kelly, 1955, p. 131)

Perhaps there is a *self-as-a-construct* as distinct from a *self-as-an-element* which has an allotted place along other construct dimensions. This self-as-construct could be that intuitive 'me-ness' or consciousness that permeates all our life. The self-as-element is a series of specific distinctions which we make between ourselves and others in particular contexts — this self is a datum which sits somewhere along many dimensions.

If there are these two types of self, then the one that is being measured in repertory grids or other techniques is not the 'uniqueness' aspect of self but some variant of the self-as-element placed on the person's construct dimensions. This idea would help account for the observation that the construct *like me in character* can be one of the most unstable in measurement terms, in contrast to the ideal self-construct (*like I'd like to be in character*), which tends to be extremely stable over time. Since the self can be viewed as an element which can be placed along many construct dimensions, it is not so surprising that in some contexts it sits on one set of dimensions and in other contexts on another set. In the context of their work a person may see themselves as forceful, a good leader and full of initiative, while in the home they might see themselves as kindly, a comforter and someone who falls in with the family wishes. A person can see themselves as a stutterer in the context of talking to people, but in more general contexts they see themselves as quite different from the group of 'stutterers'.

There is some suggestion (Smail, 1970) that a person's choice of symptom could be related to how they see themselves in relation to others. It was found that people who give more 'objective' constructs during the elicitation procedure of a repertory grid (such as *male* versus *female*; *old* versus *young*) are more likely to have somatic symptoms. In addition, previous work (Caine and Smail, 1969 and 1969a) indicates that preferences for certain types of treatment among psychiatrists and nurses depend more on their personal construing of life than on any medical arguments.

Our Selves

Most of us are aware of handling our effort to change in terms of some sort of ideal self, a picture of what we would like to be (Bannister, 1983, du Preeze, 1980). Clinical work by personal construct psychologists using forms of grid has thrown up much that is problematic for the individual about the ideal self. By getting a client to discuss or work out in grid form the meaning of constructs such as *like I am in character, like I used to be* and *like I'd like to be*, evidence can be obtained as to how persons see themselves along a time-line. For some people their construct *like I am* is almost identical with their construct *like I'd like to be* and for such people there may be relatively little force to their feelings about change. For others the distance between the self and the ideal self is so enormous that it is difficult to see how they could tackle the issue of change at all; it is as if the ideal were a kind of dream or fantasy, too far away to be converted into any kind of plan of action — being a normal weight for an obese worman, a fluent speaker for a stutterer, an Adonis for the cripple.

One way of tackling such change is to 'slot-rattle' as Kelly colourfully called it. In one such case (Fransella and Crisp, 1971) an obese woman polarised, in grid terms, from being the *opposite* of her ideal self to being *like* her ideal because she had lost a few kilogrammes in weight. This is clearly an untenable position. It seems highly likely that, for most of us, a change in one respect will not bring about a radical restructuring of our total view of ourselves; we will find we are not the great beauty, the great orator or the great athlete we thought we would be. This realisation, that the personal world has not changed radically, often leads to disillusion and hence relapse or reversion to the previous state — at least that is understood and at least we can continue to say 'if only . . .'.

For yet others, the constructs which define the self are formulated in quite different terms from the constructs in which the ideal is pictured. Thus some people see themselves as being actively concerned mainly about issues of competence, efficiency, career achievement and so forth. Yet their ideal may be couched in terms of charm, being loveable. Again change becomes problematic for such a person because there is no immediate pathway available from the present operating values to the values which represent an ultimate goal. Yet all of us seem to have to struggle in some way to relate what we have been to what we are and what we are to what we are seeking to become.

Work by Norris (1977) bears on this issue. Curiously enough her findings were foreshadowed in psychology's earlier days — days perhaps when speculation was bolder. William James (1892) proposed a simple formula for measuring self-esteem:

$$\text{self-esteem} = \frac{\text{success}}{\text{pretentions}}$$

James said of the fraction resulting from his self-esteem formula:

Such a fraction may be increased as well by diminishing the denominator as by increasing the numerator. To give up pretentions is as blessed a relief as to get them gratified; and where

> disappointment is incessant and the struggle unending this is
> what men always do . . . everything added to the Self is a
> burden as well as a pride . . . our self-feeling is in our power.

Norris (1977) studied the ideas of self of young men sentenced to
detention centres, usually for a period of two or three months. She
administered grids to these young men on arrival and on departure
and included in the grids constructs to do with self (as I am) and
ideal self. At first glance the results looked heartening. Self-
esteem seemed to have increased for 32 out of her 50 subjects in
that self and ideal self were more closely correlated in the second
grid. However, on further examination it turned out that for 82 per
cent of the detention centre trainees, who appeared to be more
closely approaching their ideal, the ideal itself had been
downgraded. They did not see themselves as 'improved' but as less
hopeful, more modest in their personal aspirations. It was as if the
detention centre, whatever its intentions, had persuaded the boys
to accept that they were pretty poor specimens and (in James's
words) to 'give up pretentions'.

Some are in no doubt about their worth and see themselves as
reflections of their ideal. Figure 7.1 shows some of the constructs
of a man convicted of several acts of arson, plotted along two
dimensions, the main one being the ideal self (Fransella and
Adams, 1966). Not only is there little discrepancy between the two
selves but these are both the very opposite of the construct *likely to
commit arson*. Arson is well recognised as an anti-social act. Yet
this arsonist seems to be saying that he, as a person, is morally
good and that people who commit arson are morally bad.

Subsequent work has demonstrated that what society construes
as undesirable or anti-social is not necessarily so construed by the
individual. For example, this seems to be the case for alcoholics
(Hoy, 1973) and stutterers (Fransella, 1968). They share the
stereotyped view of their own group but make themselves the
exception.

But it seems reasonable to assume that such dichotomies between private self construing and public interpretation are not
limited to symptoms or anti-social acts. It can be argued that most
of us will opt ourselves out of the general category of nail-biters,
hair-pullers, blushers or obsessional checkers or whatever our own
idiosyncrasy is. It can be argued that most of us will, at some time
or other, 'use' these weaknesses for our own private purposes and

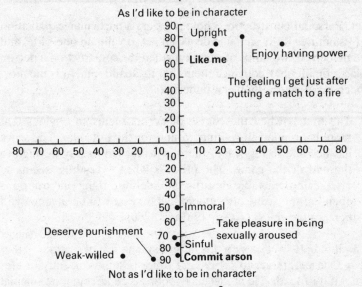

Figure 7.1: Relationship Scores (rho² × 100) Plotted Along Two Axes For Supplied and Elicited Constructs Used By An Arsonist (redrawn from Fransella and Adams, 1966)

to our own advantage, in much the same way that Tschudi (1977; 1984) sees people using 'symptoms'. In his essay 'Loaded and honest questions', he explores the way we may use symptoms as methods of manipulating other people and persuading ourselves that we are not responsible for situations which threaten us too fiercely. His central contention is that 'symptomatic behaviour is behaviour which *obliquely* gets at the issues which are important for the person'.

The Suicidal Person

Death is a threat to most of us, but not all. Krieger and colleagues (1974) talk of death-acceptors and death-fearers. Some indeed choose to die. Suicide, a lethal outcome of psychological distress, is clearly inexplicable in terms of the medical model. Biochemists who have propagandised for (though rarely discovered) physiological explanations for every kind of psychological unease have proffered no suicidococcus. Those who have seen everything mental as genetically transmitted have failed to assert an inherited gene of self-killing. Suicide seems the most ultimately personal act. Personal construct psychology offers a particular explanation of its nature. Kelly saw suicide as 'an act to validate one's life' and he perceived two kinds of occasion when the construction a person places on life may convince them that its abandonment is the most meaningful action they can undertake:

> The first is when the course of events seems so obvious that there is no point in waiting around for the outcome. The score has become so lop-sided, there is no reason to stay through to the end of the game. The other is when everything seems so utterly unpredictable that the only definite thing one can do is abandon the scene altogether. It has ceased to be a game with perceptible rules. (Kelly, 1961a, p. 260)

Landfield (1976) takes up this latter explanation of suicide — that it is a desperate act to prove that there is some certainty in life, even if it is death. He builds his hypothesis concerning the suicidal attempt on Kelly's organisation and choice corollaries. Commenting on the organisation corollary Kelly writes:

> Different constructs sometimes lead to incompatible predictions, as everyone who has experienced personal conflict is painfully aware. Man, therefore, finds it necessary to develop ways of anticipating events which transcend contradictions. (Kelly, 1955, p. 56)

Commenting on the choice corollary, he states:

> The principle of elaborative choice also includes a person's tendency to move toward that which appears to make his system more explicit and clear cut . . . this may, in some instances, appear to call for constriction of one's field — even to the point of ultimate constriction, suicide. (Kelly, 1955, p. 67)

When a particular effort at organisation fails, constriction may occur in an attempt to retain some meaning. Instead of looking outwards so as to make sense of more and more of the world, the person starts to look inward, to limit their experience and to define and restrict the construct system.

Landfield's hypothesis, based upon these two corollaries, is that suicidal behaviour will be found in the context of the disorganisation and constriction of the person's construct system. Restated, 'suicidal behaviour will occur in the context of a decreasing ability to make sense of, interpret or react to one's personal world, most importantly, a personal world of people'.

Landfield tested his ideas about suicide by giving forms of repertory grid to college students who had made serious attempts at suicide and a number of control groups including a suicidal gesture group, a 'contemplating suicide' group, a group in long-term psychotherapy, a group of hospital patients and a 'well-adjusted' group. He found that his arguments were confirmed in so far as the grids completed by the people who had made major suicidal attempts were heavily characterised by constriction (they found it simply impossible to come to conclusions about many of the people in their life, i.e. these figures were outside the range of convenience of their construct system) and by a general disorganisation of their construing.

Kelly's picture of some suicidal individuals as having concluded that 'the score has become so lop-sided that there is no reason to stay through to the end of the game' is extended by Stefan (1977) in his examination of suicide in relation to our picture of ourselves. In essence he argues that only a person who has a very rigid and constricted view of 'the game' (their lives, the world) can conclude that the outcome of the game is decided in an unalterable way. Those who view the world openly must always see 'the game' as liable to have changing fortunes, changing rules, perhaps about to become a different 'game'. Stefan defines persons from a construct theory viewpoint as either experimenters or non-experimenters. He says:

> The non-experimenting person operates from a fixed, tightly defined core structure which subsequently leads him to a reflexive view of himself as an accomplished, completed product. In contrast, the experimenter operates from a core structure less rigidly defined and more permeable, which results in a reflexive view of himself as incomplete and engaged in an ongoing process. (Stefan, 1977, p. 287)

This argument is elaborated in Stefan and Linder, 1985.

Lester (1968 and 1969) seems to follow the construct theory notion of *constriction* and points to the idea that the suicidal person's construct system may have focused down on to one issue.

The suicidal person may be seeking to validate their opinion of the world as an unfriendly and unjust place as well as their opinion of their own worthlessness. In his later study he found that suicidal individuals not only had fewer people to turn to in crisis but were more often dependent upon those they *resented*. Lester does not attempt to link these findings to the notion of hostility. However, suicide can be seen as a hostile act in Kelly's sense of the term if we accept that those who commit suicide see people on whom they are dependent as resenting *them* and they are thereby trying to extort validational evidence that this is the case — 'by killing myself I prove that they wish me dead'. Suicide has also been looked at from a personal construct perspective by Neimeyer (1984).

The Self In Confusion

One of the prime effects of carrying out research within a specific theoretical framework is that the theory decides the questions that are to be asked. A well-elaborated theory should not only provide the research with a language and a methodology but should indicate what issues are fundamental. The tie-up between a theory and the questions that one asks is obvious enough. If in England someone asks you, within ten minutes of becoming acquainted, what school you went to, you can make a reasonable inference back from that question to the kind of social theory that the questioner is walking around with: a theory which argues that type of school indicates social class membership; social class membership indicates a multitude of probable vices and virtues and so forth. Not only does theory generate issues for experimental investigation, but it asks its questions in a sequential way so that each answer elaborates a continuous and developing line of argument.

This section is devoted to a description of some long-term research into what is known as schizophrenic thought disorder, to show how personal construct theory can provide a system and a language. It should be noted that within the framework of the psychology of personal constructs 'normal' and 'abnormal' are not two psychologies, they are merely different possibilities described in the same terms.

Schizophrenic thought disorder

A thought-disordered schizophrenic once sent the following question to the BBC Brains Trust:

A Darwinian biologist in the Greco-Roman war escapes by studying Afro-Asian sociology in a Grecian way and social sciences in a Roman way; Wolfenden is the Chairman of the National Social Council. What is the future of the branch of this tree? I am an Air Force blue mouse.

While admiring the poetic qualities of the question (poetry is another form of loose construing, as is dreaming by day or by night), it can be argued that it is an unfair question.

Clinical descriptions of thought disorder stress that it is marked by vagueness, irrelevance, poverty of content and so forth and that the sum of such qualities, in the experience of the listener, is incomprehensibility. In construct theory terms, a primary question concerning 'incomprehensibility' is whether it stems from the use of a structured but private language or whether there is only a very weak language. We all accept that well-organised and systematic construct subsystems may be incomprehensible to us. Atomic physicists discoursing on the deeper mysteries of their subject may be, to most of us, incomprehensible, but we do not therefore judge them to be thought-disordered. We accept that they are probably saying something very meaningful and that it is we who lack the necessary construct subsystem to enable us to understand them. The shortcoming is ours not theirs.

Construct theory not only makes specific *meaning* versus a kind of *dreaming* a prime issue in the context of thought disorder, but also offers a mode of attack on the problem. Repertory grids, however much they may vary in content and form, are designed to show the relationship between a subject's responses in mathematical terms. They provide details of a system of categories and, quite without reference to any particular content, they can reveal organisation, or lack of it, in the person's construing. A series of experiments (Bannister, 1960; Bannister, Fransella and Agnew, 1971; McPherson *et al.*, 1973) indicated that thought-disordered schizophrenics suffer from a gross loosening of construing. This was shown by the fact that the mathematical relationships between the constructs were low and the pattern of relationships between the constructs was unstable over time — thought-disordered schizophrenics lack conceptual structure *and* consistency. In contrast, grids which were repeatedly given to groups of non-thought-disordered schizophrenics, normals, neurotics, people with brain damage, depressives and so forth, showed significantly higher relationships between constructs and the pattern of these relationships remained consistent across new grids.

A key aspect of grids in this context is that they provide us with a method of assessing degree of structure and organisation in construing without dragging us into the different issue of whether the person's construing is 'right' or 'wrong'. We do not have to make our criterion of disorder a normative one, but can separate the question of 'Does the person have an organised way of viewing his life?' from the quite different question of 'Is the subject's organised way of viewing like other people's, or is it one that I, the experimenter, deem sensible?'

The first question of *dreaming* versus *meaning* arises out of the construct theory notion of a construct *system*. A second question stems from the idea of construct *subsystems*. It is accepted that any construct has a limited range of convenience and that whole clusters of constructs are designed to deal with particular areas, for example, chemistry, theology, music, politics and so forth. A subsystem can be defined as a cluster of constructs within which high interrelationships exist while there are relatively few linkages between this and other subsystems of constructs. Theoretically at least, there is no reason to assume that one person's various subsystems will have the same structural qualities. In everyday experience most of us have encountered, say, the kind of man who has a magnificently elaborated and complex subsystem for construing motorcars, but who is barbarically simple in his construing of people.

Thus, construct theory research into schizophrenic thought disorder must, sooner or later, face the question of whether schizophrenics are disordered across their whole construct system or whether the disorder is focused. Are thought-disordered schizophrenics equally perplexed by every aspect of the world in which they live or do some kinds of things perplex them much more than others? This question was posed in a crude form by setting up an experiment to explore differences in the construing of 'people' and of 'objects' by thought-disordered schizophrenics and people with no obvious psychiatric disorder (Bannister and Salmon, 1966). Comparable grids were devised so that in the first grid the elements were photographs of people to be construed on psychological constructs such as *mean, kind* and *selfish*, while in the second grid the elements were objects (e.g. bowler hat, drawing-pin, loaf of bread) and the constructs were those whose range of convenience is objects, such as *curved-straight, cumbersome-handy, heavy-light* and so forth. Subjects completed two equivalent grids for people and two for objects so that both the degree of structure and the stability of the pattern of construct interrelationships across elements could be assessed.

The results indicated that normals construe objects in a more structured and stable way than they construe people — they are more confident as physicists than they are as psychologists. It was also found that thought-disordered schizophrenics are not as structured and stable as normals in their construing of objects. However, the greatest difference betwen the two groups lay in the discrepancy between 'object' and 'people' construing. Thought-disordered schizophrenics were only a little worse than normals in their construing of objects, but they were vastly less structured and consistent in their construing on psychological dimensions. This suggests that schizophrenic thought disorder may not be diffuse, but may be particularly related to *interpersonal* construing.

A subsequent experiment which points in the same direction, while using an entirely different technique, was carried out by Salmon, Bramley and Presly (1967). It appears that thought-disordered schizophrenics *are the equal* of non-thought-disordered schizophrenics in guessing the meaning of 'object' words from their context, but less capable in guessing the meaning of 'psychological' words. Obviously, this kind of experiment needs a great deal of replication and elaboration before we can deal with such complicating issues as 'difficulty level' (see McPherson *et al.*, 1975). However, if it is interpersonal construing that has been specifically affected in thought disorder, then any theory about its origins would have to take account of this. Theories of the 'schizococcus' would perhaps have to postulate an unlikely bug that bites 'person-thinking' rather than 'object-thinking' brain cells.

A further question arises out of the stress that personal construct psychology places on process and change. The theory is almost the exact inverse of trait theories of personality in that it specifically argues that man is a form of motion and not a static object that is occasionally kicked into movement. Thus, very rapidly, any construct theory research on thought disorder (and this would apply equally to research in other areas) is forced to face the question of how do people *become* thought-disordered. It is not enough to give an account of the condition as it stands.

The initial crude hypothesis set up for test was that thought disorder is the ultimate outcome of the experience of *serial invalidation* (having one's expectations repeatedly proved wrong). It was argued that there are a number of ways we could handle the experience of being wrong in our predictions — for example, slot change, in which we re-view the element as the contrast of our previous expectation (Jane is *hating* not *loving*); shift change, in which we attempt to reconstrue in terms of some other construct (Jane is *discourteous* rather than *courteous* and neither *hating* nor *loving*); structural change, in which links between the constructs are altered (true, Jane is *inconsiderate*, but *consideration* is not an essential part of *loving*). However, if, in spite of varying our strategies, we continue to be proved wrong in our expectations, it may be ncessary for us to loosen the links between our constructs so that our system no longer gives rise to such uni-directional, brittle and testable anticipations.

This grossly loosened construing places us in a position where we cannot, in our own terms, be wrong. It is equally true that with such a vague conceptualisation of our life, we cannot, in any very specific sense, be right either. It should be noted that loosening and tightening are not of themselves pathological reactions, but are normal reactions to varying validational fortunes. What is being argued is that thought-disordered schizophrenics have been driven to loosen *beyond the point* at which there are enough workable lines of implication between their constructs for them to re-tighten their system. They have sawn off the psychological branch on which they were sitting.

As a laboratory test of this hypothesis, experiments were conducted in which people were serially invalidated (Bannister, 1963 and 1965a). They were presented with a series of photographs and told that their judgement of personality from faces was under test. In all the experimental trials each person was presented with a group of photographs and they were asked to rank order them on a set of supplied constructs (i.e.*generous*, most to least *intelligent* and so forth). Correlations were calculated between their series of rank-orders to indicate the degree of structure implied by the ranking. In succeeding trials new sets of photographs were presented to be rank-ordered on the same set of constructs and for each trial the level of *intercorrelation* between the rankings was noted. If the subjects were in a 'serially validated' group, they were told on each occasion that their judgements were very accurate and fake life histories of the photographed people were often supplied to substantiate this. If the subjects were in a 'serially invalidated' group, they were told that they were doing badly and that their judgements were largely *inaccurate*. In some of the experiments base lines were obtained by having a 'no information' group.

The experiments showed that successively telling people they were *right* caused them to tighten their construing; the inter-correlations between their constructs rose steadily from trial to trial. Ultimately these 'right' people were putting their photographs in virtually the same order on all 'good' adjectives and in reverse order on all 'bad' adjectives — thus they were using their constructs as one single superordinate construct. Yet tightening of this type can be construed as a meaningful process. If we have an implicit theory that is working well-nigh perfectly in some area of construing, then the only change that may seem worth making is to simplify the theory and see if it works just as well. In this respect people taking part in the experiment seemed to have been following the scientific law of parsimony.

On the other hand, when the people in the experiment were successively told that they were wrong, they did not seem in the early stages to loosen the interrelationships between their constructs. But they did respond markedly with another strategy — they changed the *pattern* of interrelationships. Thus, one person completed their ninth grid to show that kind and sincere were highly positively correlated (0.70), while on the tenth grid these two constucts were shown as highly negatively correlated (−0.90). This wild swinging of the pattern of relationships between constructs seems to be an initial and marked reaction to invalidation. However, in the final experiment it was shown that if one cluster of constructs at a time rather than the whole subsystem at once was invalidated, then loosening took place. Although this is an artificial and laboratory model of the process of serial invalidation, it produced movement towards the gross loosening found in thought-disordered schizophrenics. It suggests that thought-disordered people have been wrong too often. They are like scientists whose theories have been so often disproved that they have gone out of the theory-making business.

Equally, construct theory's emphasis on process raises the question of how thought-disordered schizophrenics can again achieve ordered thinking.

An obvious initial hypothesis is that a reduction of thought disorder might take place as a result of serial *validation* (having one's expectations confirmed). Validation or invalidation happen in terms of the person's *own construct system*. This is one way in which construct theory is radically different from the notion of reinforcement theory. The traditional reinforcing cigarettes of the operant conditioning programmes would only constitute validation if the patients receiving them *personally* saw the gift of cigarettes as meaningfully linked to their own actions.

Most of what happens to thought-disordered schizophrenics interpersonally probably means little to them — in a fundamental sense it does not happen at all for them, because they have no way of making sense of it. It cannot be evidence on which they can more strongly structure their system.This meant that the programme for experimental modification of thought disorder had to begin by a very extensive search of the individual schizophrenic's construct system for dealing with people. The aim was to find some residual structure, some group of still semi-clustered constructs, some echo of a half-remembered theme, which would serve as a starting point for an elaboration of the system.

It was through this kind of residual focus that the thought-disordered schizophrenics were encouraged to 'see' people and start having expectations about them. They were then encouraged to experiment with their environment in order that they could test out the implications of their construing. Initially efforts were made to shield them from the experience of invalidation until the embryo system had begun to extend and define so that it could deal with invalidation. This research (Bannister *et al.*, 1975) produced no startling 'cure' for thought disorder but did suggest that a 'journey back' is possible, long and arduous though that journey may be.

The 'serial invalidation' hypothesis concerning the origins of schizophrenic thought disorder can be related to a number of psychological theories. In particular, it can be related to theories of the schizogenic family — theories which propose destructive family interactions as the cause of 'schizophrenia'. These include the 'double bind' hypothesis of Bateson and his co-workers (1956); arguments concerning the disintegrating effects of 'mystification' by forms of family process as put forward by Laing and Esterson (1964) and the arguments which relate schizophrenia to parental 'inculcation of confused and distorted meanings' (Lidz, 1964). All these workers see the processes resulting in 'schizophrenia' as having originated in the family.

It can be argued that these are a series of descriptions of inter-personal events which can be included in the more general concept of serial invalidation. For example, the 'double bind' situation is one in which the 'victim' subjected to the 'bind' receives two separate but conflicting messages of a kind that cannot be ignored and where the contradiction is not self-evident, for example, at its simplest level, the statement 'of course I'm not offended' delivered in a tone which says the reverse. We could argue that the person is faced with behaviour which invites two constructions either of which will be invalidated and neither of which provides any basis for effective anticipation of ensuing events.

There seem to be two difficulties with schizogenic family theories as they are usually proposed. Firstly, we may accept that the family is vital in that grossly inconsistent behaviour by parents may lead to the development of an inadequate construing system in the child. However, we do not need to base our explanation of psychological disturbances solely on the family group. There are many other social situations which may prove seriously in-validating for particular individuals. Admission to psychiatric hospital itself may provide yet a further series of invalidations. The experience of having your personal philosophy called an illness, of having strange characters insist that you make designs out of coloured blocks, of taking drugs which may produce weird sensory distortions, of being surrounded by other 'mad' people and a staff who humour you by behaving a little madly themselves, can be viewed as an impressive experiment in serial invalidation, likely to disrupt all but the most well-articulated construct system.

Secondly, schizogenic family theories tend to focus on the plight of the potential schizophrenic and the strategies which he or she is forced to adopt when victimised by his or her family. The question of why the others are behaving as they do is inadequately con-sidered. Why do double-binders double bind, mystifiers mystify and teachers of distorted meanings teach such meanings? From a construct theory viewpoint, the interpersonal situation should be considered in role relationship terms so that we can explain the behaviour of both members of a pair or all members of a relevant larger group. The problem might be looked at in terms of those role relationships (victor and vanquished, master and slave, straight-man and stooge, doctor and patient, teacher and student) which *may* demand the confusion of the one partner, in order to allow the other to define *their* clarity by contrast.

A further question about the causes of 'schizophrenia' concerns the construing strategies which may precede thought disorder. In the serial invalidation experiments the most notable initial reaction was a marked alteration in the *pattern* of construct relationships; a repeated revision of the person's idea of what characteristics went with what. The effect of such revisions on a large scale is inevitably to produce a pattern of construct relationships which is markedly idiosyncratic. The person might thus acquire unusual meanings for concepts and an 'odd' personality theory. Paranoid thinking may be of this type. The paranoid person with ideas of persecution and grandiosity may have an organised way of viewing the world, but it is a peculiar view; there is a dictionary but it is a private dictionary. If such were the case, then very serious communication difficulties would occur. The owner of the idiosyncratic system might find it very difficult to form relationships with other people or to use them as guides to their own identity — hence the essential isolation of the paranoid person.

This leaves open the question of why, if paranoia is a bus stop on the way to schizophrenic thought disorder, some get off the bus there, while others carry on to thought disorder. The answer may lie in the original state of development of the construct system at 'point of impact'. Thought disorder may be the fate of the person whose construct system had never developed beyond a relatively embryonic level, and paranoia may be the result of pressures on a construct system which was largely workable until traumatic inter-personal difficulties were met. A particular aim of this whole line of research is to help break down the global and unworkable ragbag concept of 'schizophrenia', just as the aim of broad theorising is at all times to integrate our construing.

Certainty In Chaos

While collecting the normative data for the Grid Test of Thought Disorder (Bannister and Fransella, 1966, 1967), it was observed that the structural scores for the neurotic population were very similar to the 'normal' group except for a few who construed very 'loosely'. These consisted, in the main, of those diagnosed as suffering from obsessional neurosis (characterised by the compulsion to dwell on certain themes, often resulting in repetitive and ritualistic behaviour). This seemed contrary to what one might expect, but perhaps the obsessional had so constricted their construing of the environment that the only part of their system with 'tight' structure was that to do with their obessional thoughts and acts. Subsequent clinical observations suggested that this might be so. It was as if the obsessional person was living in the only world that was meaningful to them — outside the area of their obsessions all was vagueness and confusion.

Kelly discusses this behaviour in relationship to the fragmentation corollary:

There is no clearer example of the limitation of one's ability to adjust to the vicissitudes of life, due to the impermeability of his superordinate constructs, than the case of a compulsion-neurosis client who is undergoing a marked decompensation process. The construct system of such a client is characteristically impermeable; he needs a separate pigeonhole for each new experience and he calculates his anticipation of events with minute pseudo-mathematical schemes. He has long been accustomed to subsume his principles. The variety of construction sub-systems which are inferentially incompatible with each other may, in the train of rapidly moving events, become so vast that he is hard put to it to find ready-made superordinate constructs which are sufficiently permeable or open-ended to maintain over-all consistency. He starts making new ones. (Kelly, 1955, p. 89)

Makhlouf-Norris and others (1970) provided some evidence that people, incapacitated by the overwhelming demands of their obsessional behaviour, do have fragmented interpersonal constuct subsystems. Fransella (1974) has suggested that the sequence of events leading to their desperate state might be as follows. A tightly knit core role system is one which is inadequate for dealing with invalidating evidence. When people and events continually refuse to comply with their rigid predictions, they constrict their system further.

When a person moves in the direction of constriction he tends to limit his interests, he deals with one issue at a time, he does not accept potential relationships between widely varying events, he beats out the path of his daily routine in smaller and smaller circles . . . (Kelly, 1955, p. 477).

The focusing becomes more and more confined and they are more and more desperate in their search for certainty. They must maintain control at all costs. Eventually, all they have left are small kernels of behaviour on which their whole life depends. If something undermines this one remaining area of workable construing, they have only chaos to fall back on — disintegration of their whole system — thought disorder. If this were to be the sequence of events, then the reports in the psychiatric literature that the severely obsessional individual may change category to become a thought-disordered schizophrenic are understandable. Fransella suggests, following the line of argument of this personal construct theory approach, that the obsessional should be helped to elaborate and build up constructs outside his or her symptom-based system. The aim would be to reverse the process and enlarge the range of events on which he or she can impose some meaning (Rigdon and Epting, 1983).

Construct theory research and clinical investigation in the field of psychological distress has developed considerably in recent years to include work on depression (Ashworth *et al.*, 1982, Neimeyer *et al.*, 1983, Rowe, 1983, Sheehan, 1981) anorexia (Button, 1983), alchoholism (Chambers and Sanders, 1984), agoraphobia (O'Sullivan, 1984) psychotherapy (Epting, 1984) drug dependency (Dawes, 1985) and other areas.

The Theory As Self-creator and Self-destroyer

That Kelly's theory, his vision of the person as construer, is a rich source for psychologists and a vivid challenge to many of their conventional assumptions is clear. Yet in at least three major respects the development of the theory can be judged to be inadequate or distorted.

Firstly, too great a preponderance of workers within the field of construct theory have automatically used the grid as their primary method. Repertory grid technique was a rich and brilliant extrapolation by Kelly of his theoretical insights, but its very flexibility may have delayed our development of methods and ways of exploring human experience, which might be equally appropriate.

Kelly (1961) expressed his view of the relationship between tests and theories thus:

> First of all, theoretical inventions are used to make predictions. Then, still using inventions — but of a more instrumental type, we examine the outcomes to see if there is any correspondence between what we have predicted and what our instrumentalized perceptions tell us has occurred. If we find such a correspondence we call it a discovery. We do not discover our theory; we do not discover our prediction; we do not even discover the ensuing event. What is discovered is a correspondence — a practical correspondence — between what our theoretical invention leads us to anticipate and what subsequently our *instrumental invention* leads us to observe.

Construct theory is potentially rich as an inspiration for new 'instrumental inventions', but as yet our inventiveness has only gone a little way beyond the point to which Kelly took us.

Secondly, there is the issue of the elaboration of the theory itself. So far, and understandably, the relatively small number of psychologists who have espoused personal construct psychology have seen their primary task as that of presenting and explaining the theory. This is partly a result of the very complexity of Kelly's ideas. One of the handy (and one suspects popularising) features of, say, Skinnerian theory is that it can be grasped by a bright undergraduate in about 30 minutes. Construct theory takes considerable time and examination to come to terms with. Additionally, the theory is out of keeping with many of the traditions and intellectual conventions of psychology and indeed of the popular lay philosophic stance of naïve realism. This has led us into the habit of repeated defensive exposition. The time may now have come to examine the theory critically to see what needs elaborating in its premises; to show not only that it can be, in its present form, useful and inspiring, but that it is capable of evolution.

Thirdly, we may need to guard against the temptation to dilute the theory and ignore part of its novelty and challenge in our desire to use it *readily* and make it more publicly acceptable. There is a natural tendency to use construct theory as a way of finding new answers to old and conventional questions in psychology rather than as a source for entirely new questions.

George Kelly challenged not only other extant theories in psychology but many of our deep-rooted habits of practice, for example, our reverence for large sample group discrimination designs, our assumption that the scientist-psychologist is separate from and looking down upon the 'subject', our pious belief that psychology can be scientifically value free and not have submerged political implications in almost every line of its textbooks.

In summary, the time may have come both to confront the theory and be confronted by it in a more personal and a more philosophical sense than we have hitherto ventured.

8　A PERSONAL PSYCHOLOGY

When the behaviourist observes the doings of animals, and decides whether these show knowledge or error, he is not thinking of himself as an animal, but as an at least hypothetically inerrant recorder of what actually happens. He 'knows' that animals are deceived by mirrors, and believes himself to 'know' that *he* is not being similarly deceived. By omitting the fact that *he* — an organism like any other — is observing, he gives a false air of objectivity to the results of his observation. As soon as we remember the possible fallibility of the observer, we have introduced the serpent into the behaviourist's paradise. The serpent whispers doubts, and has no difficulty in quoting scientific scripture for the purpose.

Scientific scripture, in its most canonical form, is embodied in physics (including physiology). Physics assures us that the occurrences which we call 'perceiving objects' are at the end of a long causal chain which starts from the objects, and are not likely to resemble the objects except, at best, in certain very abstract ways. We all start from 'naïve realism', that is the doctrine that things are what they seem. We think that grass is green, that stones are hard, and that snow is cold. But physics assures us that the greenness of grass, the hardness of stones, and the coldness of snow, are not the greenness, hardness, and coldness that we know in our own experience, but something very different. The observer, when he seems to himself to be observing a stone, is really, if physics is to be believed, observing the effects of the stone upon himself. Thus science seems to be at war with itself: when it most means to be objective, it finds itself plunged into subjectivity against its will. Naïve realism leads to physics, and physics, if true, shows that naïve realism is false. Therefore, naïve realism, if true, is false: therefore it is false. And therefore the behaviourist, when he thinks he is recording observations about the outer world, is really recording observations about what is happening to him. (Bertrand Russell, *An Inquiry into Meaning and Truth*, 1940)

Many people, when first confronted by personal construct theory, see it as a denial of the idea that 'reality is what it is and no amount of thinking will change it'. This point of view was prettily put by Bolingbroke (Shakespeare's *Richard II*, Act 1, Scene 3) when he had just been banished from England by the King, and his father had tried to comfort him by suggesting that he look on banishment not as an exile but as a journey of exploration, voluntarily undertaken. Bolingbroke replied:

> O, who can hold a fire in his hand
> By thinking on the frosty Caucasus?
> Or cloy the hungry edge of appetite
> By bare imagination of a feast?
> Or wallow naked in December snow
> By thinking on fantastic summer's heat?
> O, no! the apprehension of the good
> Gives but the greater feeling to the worse

Bolingbroke, in fact, is nicely supporting one of the basic contentions of personal construct psychology. He is stressing that constructs are bipolar and that if an element lies within the range of convenience of a construct then it must be most usefully seen as at one end *or* the other — it cannot be at both. The two poles of a construct have a relationship essentially of *contrast*.

But if we cannot *reverse* our view of something, this is surely not to say that we cannot *change* our view of that thing. As Kelly said, it is part of our genius that we can always *reconstrue* that which we cannot *deny*. If we go back to Gaunt's speech of comfort to his son, we will find that Bolingbroke — as is often the case with driving young men blessed with aged parents — had not listened to his father. What Gaunt had said was:

> Go, say I sent thee forth to purchase honour,
> And not the King exil'd thee; or suppose
> Devouring pestilence hangs in our air
> And thou art flying to a fresher clime.
> Look what thy soul holds dear, imagine it
> To lie that way thou goest, not whence thou com'st
> Suppose the singing birds musicians,
> The grass whereon thou tread'st the presence strew'd
> The flowers fair ladies, and thy steps no more

Than a delightful measure or a dance;
For gnarling sorrow hath less power to bite
The man that mocks at it and sets it light.

Gaunt is here opposing a pre-emptive construction of
Bolingbroke's situation. He is arguing that although Bolingbroke's
life abroad may be a banishment, it need not be viewed as *nothing
but* a banishment. It can be viewed as a grand tour and an
opportunity to explore new delights.

Very often psychotherapists find themselves playing Gaunt to a
neurotic Bolingbroke. Neurotics who are convinced that they are
villains and the rest of mankind saints begin by assuming that
whatever new idea you suggest, or new personal venture you urge
them to undertake, amounts to nothing more than the contrary
assertion that they are saints and the rest of the world villains.
Indeed it is by no means impossible to get them to polarise and see
themselves and others in this reversed light. But it is very difficult
to convince neurotics that perhaps the *villain-saint* dichotomy itself
is not a useful one and that there may be entirely different ways of
construing, constructs at 90 degrees to their favourite, which might
open up novel possibilities.

The Personal Relevance of Construct Theory

Much has been made of the reflexive quality of personal construct
psychology. It has been argued that it is a theory about theories,
that it treats scientists as people and people as scientists. It has
been argued that in this respect it differs sharply from traditional
psychological theories which do not comment on their makers as
part of their subject-matter.

> Psychologists share the privilege of scientists in being outside
> the range of convenience of such theories. Granted, at a joke
> level psychologists may argue that a particular psycho-analyst is
> writing a particular paper in order to sublimate his sex instinct
> or we may toy with the notion that a book by some learning
> theorist is evidence that the said learning theorist was suffering
> from a build-up of reactive inhibition. But in our more solemn
> moments we seem to prefer the paradoxical view that
> psychologists are explainers, predictors and experimenters,

whereas the organism, God bless him, is a very different kettle of fish.

In short, we have not yet faced up to the issue of reflexivity and the need for reflexivity in psychological thinking. If we are going to make so bold as to utter such statements as 'thinking is a matter of A and B and a little C', then such statements should equally subsume the thinking which led to them. If we are going to climb up on to platforms and make generalizations about human behaviour, then such generalizations should clearly explain the behaviour of climbing up on to platforms and making generalizations about human behaviour. The delight and instruction which many of us find in George Kelly's Personal Construct Theory derives in no small measure from the fact that it is an explicitly reflexive theory. There may be no onus on the chemist when he writes his papers on the nature of acids and alkalis to account in terms of his acid-alkali distinction for his behaviour in writing a journal paper. But psychologists are in no such fortunate position.

Turning this issue of reflexivity the other way around, I am reminded of a recurrent theme in certain types of science fiction story. The master-chemist has finally produced a bubbling green slime in his test tubes, the potential of which is great but the properties of which are mysterious. He sits alone in his laboratory, test tube in hand, brooding about what to do with the bubbling green slime. Then it slowly dawns on him that the bubbling green slime is sitting alone in the test tube brooding about what to do with him. This special nightmare of the chemist is the permanent work-a-day world of the psychologist — the bubbling green slime is always wondering what to do about you. (Bannister, 1966, pp. 21-2)

If we claim that construct theory comments intelligently on the processes of the very psychologist who uses it, we are claiming that it would comment intelligently on the processes of all of us — for we are all, of necessity, psychologists.

Consider the implications of the idea of *tightening* and *loosening* as a cyclic process, essential to personal development. Most of us grudgingly acknowledge that we sometimes loosen and sometimes tighten. We dream and we plan, we are fanciful and we are logical, we are humorous and we are serious, we see the world as sometimes strangely magical and sometimes as just a collection of routine facts, we treat each other as if we all have mysterious possibilities and also as if we fit neatly into hard and fast, practical roles. Yet we do not always recognise that each of these is a phase necessary to the other. Dreams give birth to plans and the realising of plans gives birth to further dreams.

Just as many psychologists have opted permanently for a tight or a loose psychology, so many of us seem personally to have taken up residence at some fixed point in what should be a cycle. It is as if we type-cast ourselves in a general way as being *either* Cavalier or Roundhead, *either* tender-minded or tough-minded, *either* romantic or classic, *either* Koestler's Yogi or Koestler's Commissar. And for people who choose tightness or looseness as a basic posture towards life, the choice has the force of a moral decision. The orderly and materialist and practical look with contempt on lives they see as half-baked and self-indulgent. The sensitive and lyrical and passionate are appalled by those they see as rule-bound and mercenary. If we mistake repetition for consistency and assumptions for reality, then we can quite easily transmute what should be different phases of living into different kinds of person. And in so doing, we do not just impoverish our personal lives, we lend support to a social history which has tended to enforce these same crippling choices. Consider merely the way in which men and women have been moulded into being 'masculine' and 'feminine' respectively and consider how much this has deducted from the achievements and imagination of both (cf. Fransella and Frost, 1977).

Answers Beget Questions

Orthodox psychologists seem to share one crucial assumption which is utterly unacceptable from a construct theory point of view. This is the assumption that humanity has *a nature* which we might eventually fathom and that will be that. Personal construct psychology does not simply argue that it will be very difficult to fathom the nature of humanity — most psychologists would admit that. It argues that it is a meaningless ideal, since the nature of individual people and of humanity is evolving and therefore can never be finally explained by any theory. The very theories which psychologists elaborate are part of this evolution, yet some quaintly think that the journeying spirit we call a person will stay still until the psychologist's work is done.

Kelly (1969) phrased it succinctly:

Behaviour is a man's way of changing his circumstances, not proof that he has submitted to them. What on earth, then, can present day psychology be thinking about when it says that it intends only to predict and control behaviour scientifically? Does it intend to halt the human enterprise in its tracks?

He went on to reflect on those immutable laws of behaviour:

There are, indeed, moments when I deeply suspect that man's only purpose in discovering the laws of human behaviour is to contrive some way to escape them. (Kelly, 1969)

But if we are to take this process view of people and see them as continually posing questions and finding answers, then we must recognise that there will be new questions inherent in the newly found answer. The new perception and the new act which are a solution for an old problem contain in their newness the elements of our next problem.

Consider this argument as a way of looking at the curious dispute between behaviourists and psychoanalysts about 'symptom substitution'. Both behaviourists and psychoanalysts, being good, normatively minded folk, are prepared to call certain things that people do 'symptoms', which makes it clear that, regardless of what the behaviour might mean for the person, it is going to have to be got rid of. However, behaviourists regard the 'symptom' as a maladaptive learned habit which can be unlearned and thereby utterly dispensed with. The psychoanalysts on the other hand regard the 'symptom' as a function of the person's faulty psychodynamics. They argue that if it is got rid of, without altering the nature of these psychodynamics, it will be replaced by another 'symptom' which will play the same part in the person's psychological economy. From a personal construct point of view, these are both very strange contentions. When a person has solved one of their problems, or to keep them in their proper station let us say we have cured them of one of their symptoms, they inevitably acquire the problems resulting from that solution. But these are not simply 'substitutions', they may well represent a substantial forward step in the personal evolution of the 'patient'. It is equally true that they *are* related to the previous 'symptom'. Consider an actual case.

The young man had a phobia about telephones and travelling. About a year of desensitisation treatment enabled him to travel and use the telephone. He commented on the utter pointlessness of such an achievement since he had no one to ring up and no one to travel to. He had formed no relationships with his fellows. After two years of psychotherapeutic exploration and experimentation, the young man was going to social gatherings, visiting his newly found friends, was a member of this or that hobbies group. He then pointed out that no one could care less than he did for the kind of superficial social chit-chat relationships, mainly with men, which he now formed in great numbers. What he wanted was a deep, passionate, intense, sexual and exclusive relationship with a woman. And so he began . . . now are we to argue that the sequential problems were no more than magical substitutes for his earlier problems or for that matter see no connection between them?

So, at a personal level, if we try to make use of construct theory, we may range it alongside a number of sources of wisdom, which teach us that we can always reconstrue but that we must accept responsibility for our new constructions and for the new mysteries which they will generate.

The Psychological Experiment

If, as psychologists, we could forget the dreams that came with our first chemistry set, that we would ultimately be absolutely precise, Nobel prize-winning, pioneering, socially accredited scientists of the kind that foreign governments would think it worthwhile to kidnap, that we might stop trying to mimic what we conceive to be the standard experiments of physics and begin to consider what a truly psychological experiment might be like. Even if we retain our focus on classical experiments in the natural sciences, we might pay less attention to their mathematical precision and more to their quality as acts of imagination. The vast majority of formal psychological experiments could win prizes for being exquisitely obsessional or the apotheosis of the platitude, but they could hardly be called acts of imagination. Most of them were born out of the literature and, no doubt, will be buried in it.

Suppose we were to begin experimenting *with* individuals instead of *on* individuals. Suppose we were to accept that, however formal and systematic the psychological experiment, it ought to be more kin to the kinds of experiments which novelists undertake with their readers, or children undertake with their parents, or lovers undertake with each other, than the kind of experiments which were undertaken by the stereotypical Victorian physicist who seems to be our current ideal. What sort of experiments might we then find ourselves engaged in? It is certain that initially they would be rather murky and quite unpublishable, but these two conditions might be no bad thing in themselves. Consider some moves in this direction (Bannister, 1981).

McFall (1965) played with a form of experiment which earned itself the title of McFall's Mystical Monitor. The procedure was simple enough. You take a person (he or she is not a 'subject', they are also 'experimenters') and you isolate him or her with a tape recorder and a set of suggestions. The suggestions are that they set the tape recorder running and begin to talk into it — talking about whatever comes into their heads. After a period of 20 minutes or so they are to rewind the tape and play back what was said. Then they are to begin again and talk into the tape for an hour or as long as they like. Then they are to rewind and play through what was said this time. They can if they wish play it through two or three times, but the key point is that when they have finished they *must* erase the tape completely so that no record is left.

Obviously this is a variant on the time-honoured custom of talking to oneself. But the gimmick of the tape adds the extra dimension of listening to oneself. And the essence of the talk is that it is talk *without an audience*. This is the reason for the first 20 minute run which has to be listened to before the main session begins. Almost invariably people report that they were embarrassed by the first 20 minutes because they heard themselves talking *as to an audience*; they heard themselves posturing and presenting themselves, excusing themselves, concealing them-selves, doing all the necessary things that we do when we have any kind of audience. But many found that listening to that first 20 minutes or so forced them into asking the inevitable question — something like 'who do I think I am kidding?'. And since they obviously were not kidding anybody, they found that the next long section of the tape represented something new — perhaps a chance to reflect on their own reflections. The absolute guarantee, made to oneself, that the tape will be erased is essential or the tape will be merely a speech to some future audience, perhaps a future self.

What were the results of McFall's experiments?. From an orthodox point of view perhaps there were not really any 'results' at all. Certainly none that could be rushed into the journals at the 5 per cent level of confidence. But if we rephrase the question and say *what was learned from the experiment*, then the answer is quite a lot. Most of the experimenters (and again the answer to the subject-experimenter identity question is that everyone who does this is an experimenter) claimed they had learned something from it about the issues in their life. Even though the very nature of the experiment (not accidentally) meant the destruction of much of the 'data', it was possible systematically to collect and analyse the views of those who had undertaken the experiment and see what sort of conclusions were forthcoming. It might be possible to frame the process into a more formal experiment (perhaps of a laddering type) within a theoretical framework, with hypotheses and with accountable conclusions about the fate of the hypotheses. But perhaps the most important 'result' of this kind of venture is that it may make us look in new directions without being too desperate to freeze what we see into a technology.

But curiously enough, if we make technology truly our technique and not our framework, then just as we can make the complex mathematics of grid method serve the expression of the individual, so we can make the overweight expertise of the computer serve the purposes of McFall's Mystical Monitor. Thomas and Harri-Augstein (1985) have developed ways in which people may talk to themselves using as their sounding board the language of repertory grid technique programmed into a computer. The 'subjects' (the problem of who is running the show and on whose behalf it is all being undertaken arises yet again) sit down at the computer, which begins to ask them questions about how their bookie and their wife/husband are alike and thereby different from their boss. They go on 'telling' the computer their views of people in their world (or their differential evaluations of wines or films or towns or computer programs).

The computer stores and continually analyses this information and feeds the results of the analysis to the 'subject'. Thus, they are no longer simply hearing what they have said, but having some of the implications of what they said worked out for them. They may be told what the relationships between their constructs are, or which people they seem to have great difficulty in understanding. (The continuing grid analysis reveals the pattern of combinations of qualities which a person sees as going together and it is therefore easy to see which people in a person's world are 'psychological impossibilities' — they are alleged to possess a combination of qualities contrary to the pattern, being, say, selfish and generous, clever and idiotic.) Eventually the computer may offer choice points. Subjects can decide whether they want to go on and define more clearly a familiar part of their world or try to sort out some new aspects of their life (the 'extension or definition' of the choice corollary). Or two persons may 'consult' the computer together and be told something of their ways of understanding and misunderstanding each other.

Once again, we are faced with the problem of what are the 'results' of this kind of experiment? If people choose not to wipe out the record of their transactions with the computer, then certainly there are quantified data in abundance and from it we might discover much about the process of construing in *real time* terms. For example, we might learn something on that very issue of why do we sometimes choose to define and at other times opt to extend our understanding. But again, perhaps the most important immediate implications of this line of research have to do with the level at which it lets the person work and the level at which we try to understand what the person has been doing.

There are ways in which people can formalise and analyse their own interplay without a computer. Mair (1970 and 1970a) has suggested that, instead of using a physics model to guide us in designing experiments, we look to the technique which people most often use to investigate and experiment with each other — the conversation. Experiments designed in terms of a conversational model might take the form of a kind of cycle of inquiry such as he describes in the following passage:

Consider a practical situation. Mr Rogers and Mr Skinner sit down together to undertake an exploratory study of how they each and together 'theorize' and 'experiment' about themselves, each other and others in general. Mr Skinner writes *two* brief character sketches of Mr Rogers (following, perhaps, similar instructions to those used by Kelly for Self-Characterizations). One of these sketches is written *only for himself*; a completely private view of Mr Rogers which no one else will see. The other sketch is written *specifically* for Mr Rogers to read. This latter one is couched in terms and touches on topics which Mr Skinner will feel *quite comfortable* about telling Mr Rogers, he is not required to 'bare his soul' or 'tell all', but just to give a picture of his view of Mr Rogers which he will feel quite able to take (one participant must not traumatize the other or others since each needs everyone else to stay around so that the inquiry can continue).

Mr Rogers also writes two equivalent sketches about Mr Skinner, one private for his own eyes only and the other a more public one specifically for Mr Skinner to read.

Messrs Skinner and Rogers now *pass to the other* their 'public' sketches. They read them, then systematically take turns at questioning the other to clarify points in the sketch they received which they understood little or not at all. They then take time to *note down* their initial reactions to the new information which has been given them about themselves; what they feel, think, want to do, say, reject, accept, avoid or welcome about it.

Next, in turn, each questions the other in detail about what *evidence* he has for each of the statements he has made about the other; about his grounds for believing the things he does and for saying the things he has; about the criteria he may be functioning in terms of, in accepting the evidence he has done and about the criteria and evidence he would use if he were to become more certain yet of the validity of the statements he has made. In addition, at this stage, they may then examine the description of themselves presented to them by the other and analyse it in terms of what it seems to suggest about the inter- ests, ideas, strengths, limitations, tactics and such like *of the person who wrote it*. Each will then also take turns in questioning the other concerning the evidence which justifies the conclusions he has reached regarding the characteristics and concerns of the writer. (Here, as at any other point in the entire investigation, each may write both public and private versions of conclusions reached, the evidence he has used, the assessments he has made, and so forth.)

At this point the first face to face encounter might end and each withdraw to continue their normal lives, arranging to meet again in an hour, day, week or month (whatever their purpose in the inquiry) to continue the face to face part of the study. As they go, however, the study goes with them. In the encounter just completed many personal issues will have been touched on and stirred; each participant (and there could easily be more than two) may find, whether he wishes it or not, that he continues to ruminate on, act out, experiment with, attempt to disconfirm or confirm in a variety of imaginary or practical ways some of the issues and possibilities raised. Each participant must be vigilant to note down at any time how he goes about dealing with these matters (and this is likely to require considerable training in sensitive, detached self-awareness).

The cycle of encounter and withdrawal for personal exploration can be repeated indefinitely or terminated at any agreed stage, depending on the main point of the study or the concerns of those involved. (Mair, 1970, pp. 170-1)

Mair (1977) went on to develop a notion of self not as a simple entity but as a 'community of self' and then to explore the way in which we use metaphor as a way of extending outsleves (Mair, 1977a).

Looking at the suggested procedure we are faced again by the same problems (or are they solutions?) which we saw in relation to the two earlier ventures. Who are the experimenters and who are the subjects? What about the data which by its very nature will not become public property? And where have all the statistics gone? And what about the 'results'? On the last question we can see the kind of issues on which this sort of experiment might throw light. What are we to make of any discrepancy between my portrait of you for you and my portrait of you which I feel I must keep to myself? Are we to take the barren view that it is a measure of the extent to which I lie? Or could we see it perhaps as the beginnings of a way to measure the nature of the role relationship between you and me?

And suppose — as Mair suggests — we add in other viewpoints, such as how I view myself for myself or how we view each other later, after we have been through the cycle once. Might not content analyses of yet further differences between these viewpoints reveal something about the ways in which we go about handling evidence or the degree to which others can see us in our own terms?

Pondering the question of 'results' inevitably leads us to the interesting construct of replicability, for psychologists talk much of replication and revere it as a defining characteristic of science. What does replicability mean in experimental psychology? It does not mean that there is any likelihood that our experiments will be exactly repeated, for this is a fantastically rare event. It seems to mean that we have designed and presented them in such a way that they *could* be repeated. Presumably this is not for some tricksy reason such as reassuring others that we have not lied about our results. It seems more likely that replicability is a discipline we impose upon ourselves to make sure that the way we have defined our experimental operations is clear enough to communicate itself reliably to other psychologists.

This is fine, but let us acknowledge that what is thereby rendered relatively clear are the *operational procedures* of the experiment. The theoretical argument, that which the whole experiment was about, may still be painfully vague. There may be no real agreement about what it all means, only a disagreement concealed by our happy unity about the definition of the operational procedures. We may be agreed as to what we mean by rate of shitting in the rat, we may even be agreed that we will refer to this as an operational definition of 'emotionality', but we have not thereby come to any sort of agreement as to what, in the long run and in all its glory, 'emotionality' is going to be taken to mean.

In terms of this view of replicability, are the kinds of experiment foreshadowed by the conversational model procedures likely to prove susceptible to 'replication'? If a large number of experimenters undertake such procedures (giving us genuine multiple replication), then they can state the conclusions they have drawn in formal and general terms. If we find indentifiable themes repeated in these conclusions, we may be able to examine them by alternative procedures in new contexts. Then, may we not have achieved the kind of commonality and basis for useful, continuing scientific argument that is normally sought for under the rubric replicability? Certainly it would be better to find the answer to such a question by conducting experiments of this kind, rather than ignoring them because they do not fit the narrowest possible interpretation put on the Science Club rules. Thereby, we might resolve the mastery-mystery complex which Bakan (1967) sees us as suffering from and find that some very fine experiments were labelled psychotherapy (Agnew, 1985).

A Perspective For Psychology

There is evidence that pure data-grubbing and common sense eclecticism are already diminishing styles in psychology, though the need for quick pay-off and publication, and a longing for personal 'security' and publicly demonstrable 'achievement' may maintain these traditions for a while longer. Most psychologists seem to be moving on from accepting Popper's dictum about the need for our hypotheses to be falsifiable to accepting his more extensive definition of science as essentially a line of argument — and a line of argument that needs an integrated language if it is not to be continually derailed. Theory is a necessary *basis* for scientific endeavour, not the end product of fact-gathering or icing to be added when the real business of cake-baking is over. Popper discussed this in the following terms:

> Thus the real situation is quite different from the one visualized by the naive empiricist, or the believer in inductive logic. He thinks that we begin by collecting and arranging our experiences, and so ascend the ladder of science. Or to use the more formal mode of speech, that if we wish to build up a science, we have first to collect protocol sentences. But if I am ordered: 'record what you are now experiencing' I shall hardly know how to obey this ambiguous order. Am I to report that I am writing: that I hear a bell ringing: a newsboy shouting: a loudspeaker droning: or am I to report, perhaps, that the noises irritate me? And even if the order could be obeyed: however rich a collection of statements might be assembled in this way, it could never add up to a science. A science needs points of view and theoretical problems. (Popper, 1959)

In passing we might note that Popper's picture of scientists as proceeding by refuting their own conjectures is quite a neat description, from a construct theory viewpoint, of how we extend our personal lives.

But a further necessary development in our perspective of a science of psychology has to do with questions such as how does a *science* of psychology relate to our personal psychologies? What of the political and social value problems implicit in trying to develop a science of psychology? What are the limits of detachment and objectivity? Do psychologists talk to the wrong people in deferring to colleagues in the natural sciences and would they do better to consort with artists, theologians, historians, lawyers, and so forth. These are questions which psychologists seem rarely to consider.

The aim of science is conventionally stated to be prediction and control. The aim of personal construct psychology, put at its most pious, is liberation through *understanding*. A construct theorist sees prediction not as an aim, but as a means of putting our understanding to the test. Control, in any real sense, should not be an aim. It is a dangerous myth.

APPENDIX

Formal Content of Personal Construct Theory

Fundamental postulate: A person's processes are psychologically channellised by the ways in whch they anticipate events.

Construction corollary: A person anticipates events by construing their replications.

Individuality corollary: Persons differ from each other in their constructions of events.

Organisation corollary: Each person characteristically evolves, for their convenience in anticipating events, a construction system embracing ordinal relationships between constructs.

Dichotomy corollary: A person's construction system is composed of a finite number of dichotomous constructs.

Choice corollary: Persons choose for themselves that alternative in a dichotomised construct through which they anticipate the greater possibility for the elaboration of their system.

Range corollary: A construct is convenient for the anticipation of a finite range of events only.

Experience corollary: A person's construction system varies as they successively construe the replication of events.

Modulation corollary: The variation in a person's construction system is limited by the permeability of the constructs within whose range of convenience the variants lie.

Fragmentation corollary: A person may successively employ a variety of construction systems which are inferentially incompatible with each other.

Commonality corollary: To the extent that one person employs a construction of experience which is similar to that employed by another, their processes are psychologically similar to those of the other person.

Sociality corollary: To the extent that one person construes the construction processes of another, they may play a role in a social process involving the other person.

Formal Aspects of Constructs

Range of convenience: A construct's range of convenience comprises all those things to which the user would find its application useful.

Focus of convenience: A construct's focus of convenience comprises those particular things to which the user would find its application maximally useful. These are the elements upon which the construct is likely to have been formed originally.

Elements: The things or events which are abstracted by a person's use of a construct are called elements. In some systems these are called objects.

Context: The context of a construct comprises those elements among which the user ordinarily discriminates by means of the construct. It is somewhat more restricted than the range of convenience, since it refers to the circumstances in which the construct emerges for practical use and not necessarily to all the circumstances in which a person might eventually use the construct. It is somewhat more extensive than the focus of convenience, since the construct may often appear in circumstances where its application is not optimal.

Pole: Each construct discriminates between two poles, one at each end of its dichotomy. The elements abstracted are like each other at each pole with respect to the construct and are unlike the elements at the other pole.

Contrast: The relationship between the two poles of a construct is one of contrast.

Likeness end: When referring specifically to elements at one pole of a construct, one may use the term 'likeness end' to designate that pole.

Contrast end: When referring specifically to elements at one pole of a construct, one may use the term 'contrast end' to designate the opposite pole.

Emergence: The emergent pole of a construct is that one which embraces most of the immediately perceived context.

Implicitness: The implicit pole of a construct is that one which embraces contrasting context. It contrasts with the emergent pole. Frequently the person has no available symbol or name for it; it is symbolised only implicitly by the emergent term.

Symbol: An element in the context of a construct which represents not only itself but also the construct by which it is abstracted by the user is called the construct's symbol.

Permeability: A construct is permeable if it admits newly perceived elements to its context. It is impermeable if it rejects elements on the basis of their newness.

Constructs Classified According To The Nature of Their Control Over Their Elements

Pre-emptive construct: A construct which pre-empts its elements for membership in its own realm exclusively is called a pre-emptive construct. This is the 'nothing but' type of construction — 'if this is a ball it is nothing but a ball'.

Constellatory construct: A construct which fixes the other realm membership of its elements is called a constellatory construct. This is stereotyped or typological thinking.

Propositional construct: A construct which carries no implications regarding the other realm membership of its elements is a propositional construct. This is uncontaminated construction.

General Diagnostic Constructs

Preverbal constructs: A preverbal construct is one which continues to be used, even though it has no consistent word symbol. It may or may not have been devised before the client had command of speech symbolism.

Submergence: The submerged pole of a construct is the one which is less available for application to events.

Suspension: A suspended element is one which is omitted from the context of a construct as a result of revision of the client's construct system.

Level of cognitive awareness: The level of cognitive awareness ranges from high to low. A high-level construct is one which is readily expressed in socially effective symbols; whose alternatives are both readily accessible; which falls well within the range of convenience of the client's major construction; and which is not suspended by its superordinating constructs.

Dilation: Dilation occurs when a person broadens their perceptual field in order to reorganise it on a more comprehensive level. It does not, in itself, include the comprehensive reconstruction of those elements.

Constriction: Constriction occurs when a person narrows their perceptual field in order to minimise apparent incompatibilities.

Comprehensive constructs: A comprehensive construct is one which subsumes a wide variety of events.

Incidental constructs: An incidental construct is one which subsumes a narrow variety of events.

Superordinate constructs: A superordinate construct is one which includes another as one of the elements in its context.

Subordinate constructs: A subordinate construct is one which is included as an element in the context of another.

Regnant constructs: A regnant construct is a kind of superordinate construct which assigns each of its elements to a category on an all-or-none basis, as in classical logic. It tends to be non-abstractive.

Core constructs: A core construct is one which governs a person's maintenance processes.

Peripheral constructs: A peripheral construct is one which can be altered without serious modification of the core structure.

Tight constructs: A tight construct is one which leads to unvarying predictions.

Loose constructs: A loose construct is one which leads to varying predictions but which retains its identity.

Constructs Relating to Transition

Threat: Threat is the awareness of an imminent comprehensive change in one's core structures.

Fear: Fear is the awareness of an imminent incidental change in one's core structures.

Anxiety: Anxiety is the awareness that the events with which one is confronted lie mostly outside the range of convenience of one's construct system.

Guilt: Guilt is the awareness of dislodgement of the self from one's core role structure.

Aggressiveness: Aggressiveness is the active elaboration of one's perceptual field.

Hostility: Hostility is the continued effort to extort validational evidence in favour of a type of social prediction which has already been recognised as a failure.

CPC cycle: The CPC Cycle is a sequence of construction involving in succession, circumspection, pre-emption and control, leading to a choice precipitating the person into a particular situation.

Creativity Cycle: The Creativity Cycle is one which starts with loosened construction and terminates with tightened and validation construction.

REFERENCES

ADAMS-WEBBER, J. R. (1969) 'Cognitive complexity and sociality', *Brit. J. soc. clin. Psychol.*, *8*, 211-16
——, (1970) 'An analysis of the discriminant validity of several repertory grid indices', *Brit. J. Psychol.*, *61*, 83-90
——, (1979) *Personal Construct Theory*, Wiley
——, and MIRC, E. (1976) Assessing the development of student teachers' role conceptions', *Brit. J. ed. Psychol.*, *46*, 338-40
AGNEW, J. (1985) 'Childhood disorders' in E. Button (ed.), *Personal Construct Theory and Mental Health*, Croom Helm, London
——, and BANNISTER, D. (1973) 'Psychiatric diagnosis as a psuedo-specialist language', *Brit. J. med. Psychol.*, *46*, 69-73
ALLPORT, G. W. (1937) *Personality: a Psychological Interpretation*, Holt, Rinehart & Winston, Eastbourne
——, (1964) 'The fruits of eclecticism — bitter or sweet?', *Acta Psychol.*, *23*, 27-44
APPLEBEE, A. N. (1975) 'Developmental changes in consensus in construing within a specified domain', *Brit. J. Psychol.*, *66*, 473-80
——, (1976) 'The development of children's responses to repertory grids', *Brit. J. soc. clin. Psychol.*, *15*, 101-2
ARGYLE, M. (1969) *Social Interaction*, Methuen, London
——, SALTER, V., NICHOLSON, H., WILLIAMS, M. and BURGESS, P. (1970) 'The communication of inferior and superior attitudes by verbal and non-verbal signals', *Brit. J. soc. clin. Psychol.*, *9*, 222-31
ARGYRIS, C. (1969) 'The incompleteness of social-psychological theory: examples from small group, cognitive consistency and attribution research', *Amer. Psychol.*, *24*, 893-908
ASCH, S. E. (1951) 'Effects of group pressure upon the modification and distortion of judgement' in H. Guetzkow.(ed.), *Groups, Leadership and Men*, Carnegie Press
ASHWORTH, C. M., BLACKBURN, I. M., AND MCPHERSON, F. M. (1982) 'The performance of depressed and manic patients on some repertory grid measures: a cross-sectional study', *Brit. J. med. Psychol.*, *55*, 247-55
BAILLIE-GROHMAN, R. (1975) 'The use of a modified form of repertory grid technique to investigate the extent to which deaf school leavers tend to use stereotypes', unpublished M.Sc. diss., London University
BAKAN, D. (1967) *On Method: Toward a Reconstruction of Psychological Investigation*, Jossey-Bass,
BAKER, R. (1979) 'Orthographic awareness' in U. Frith (ed.), *Cognitive Processes in Spelling*, Academic Press,
BALOFF, N. and BECKER, S. W. (1967) 'On the futility of aggregating individual learning curves', *Psychol. Reports*, *20*, 183-91
BANNISTER, D. (1959) 'An application of personal construct theory (Kelly) to schizoid thinking', unpublished Ph.D. thesis, London University
——, (1960) 'Conceptual structure in thought-disordered schizophrenics', *J. ment. Sci.*, *106*, 1230-49
——, (1962) 'Personal construct theory: a summary and experimental paradigm', *Acta Psychol.*, *20*, 104-20
——, (1962a) 'The nature and measurement of schizophrenic thought disorder', *J.ment.Sci.*, *108*, 825-42

175

——, (1963) 'The genesis of schizophrenic thought disorder: a serial invalidation hypothesis', *Brit. J. Psychiat.*, *109*, 680

——, (1965) 'The rationale and clinical relevance of repertory grid technique', *Brit.J.Psychiat.*, *111*, 977-82

——, (1965a) 'The genesis of schizophrenic thought disorder: re-test of the serial invalidation hypothesis', *Brit. J. Psychiat.*, *111*, 377-82

——, (1966) 'Psychology as an exercise in paradox', *Bull. Brit. J. Psychol. Soc.*, *19*, 21-6

——, (1968) 'The myth of physiological psychology', *Bull. Brit. Psychol. Soc.*, *21*, 229-31

——, (1970) 'Science through the looking glass' in D. Bannister (ed.), *Perspectives in Personal Construct Theory*, Academic Press

——, (1970a) (ed.) *Perspectives in Personal Construct Theory*, Academic Press,

——, (1970b) 'Comment on explanation and the concept of personality by H. J. Eysenck' in R. Borger and F. Cioffi (eds.), *Explantion in the Behavioural Sciences*, Cambridge University Press

——, (1970c) 'Psychological theories as ways of relating to people', *Brit. J. med. Psychol.*, *43*, 241-4

——, (1975) 'Personal construct psychotherapy' in D. Bannister (ed.), *Approaches in the Psychological Therapies*, Wiley, Chichester

——, (1977) 'The logic of passion', in D. Bannister (ed.), *New Perspectives in Personal Construct Theory*, Academic Press

——, (1977a) (ed.), *New Perspectives in Personal Construct Theory*, Academic Press

——, (1981) 'The fallacy of animal experimentation in psychology' in D. Sperlinger (ed.), *Animals in Research: New Perspectives in Animal Experimentation*, Wiley, Chichester

——, (1981a) 'Personal construct theory and research method' in P. Reason and J. Rowan (eds.), *Human Enquiry*, Wiley, Chichester

——, (1983) 'Self in personal construct theory' in J. Adams-Webber and J. Mancuso (eds.), *Applications of Personal Construct Theory*, Academic Press, Toronto

——, (1985) 'The patient's point of view' in D. Bannister (ed.), in *Issues and Approaches in Personal Construct Theory*, Academic Press, London

——, ADAMS-WEBBER, J. R., PENN, W. I. and RADLEY, A. R. (1975) 'Reversing the process of thought disorder: a serial validation experiment', *Brit. J. soc. clin. Psychol.*, *14*, 169-80

——, and AGNEW, J. (1977) 'The child's construing of self' in A. W. Landfield (ed.), *Nebraska Symposium on Motivation 1976*, University of Nebraska Press, Lincoln

——, and BOTT, M. (1973) 'Evaluating the person' in P. Kline (ed.), *New Approaches in Psychological Measurement*, Wiley

——, and FRANSELLA, F. (1966) 'A grid test of schizophrenic thought disorder', *Brit. J. soc. clin. Psychol.*, *5*, 95-102. Also in Psychological Test Publications, Barnstaple (1967)

——, FRANSELLA, F. and AGNEW, J. (1971) 'Characteristics and validity of the grid test of thought disorder', *Brit. J. soc. clin. Psychol.*, *10*, 144-51

——, and MAIR, J. M. M. (1968) *The Evaluation of Personal Constructs*, Academic Press

——, and SALMON, P. (1966) 'Schizophrenic thought disorder: specific or diffuse', *Brit. J. med. Psychol.*, *39*, 215-19

——, and SALMON, P. (1967) 'Measures of superordinacy', unpublished study

BARTLETT, F. C. (1932) *Remembering*, Cambridge University Press

BARTON, E. S., WALTON, T. and ROWE, D. (1976) 'Using grid technique with the mentally handicapped' in P. Slater (ed.), *Explorations of Intrapersonal Space*, Wiley

BATESON, G., JACKSON D., HALEY, J. and WEAKLAND, J. (1956) 'Toward a theory of schizophrenia', *Behavioural Science*, *1*, 251-64
BEAIL, N. (1985) (ed.), *Repertory Grid Technique and Personal Constructs: Applications in Clinical and Educational Settings*, Croom Helm, London
BECK, A. T. (1976) *Cognitive Therapy and the Emotional Disorders*, International Universities Press, New York
BEECH, H. R. and FRANSELLA, F. (1968) *Research and Experiment in Stuttering*, Pergamon Press, Oxford
BENDER, M. P. (1968) 'Does construing people as similar involve similar behaviour towards them?', *Brit. J. soc. clin. Psychol.*, *7*, 303-4
——, (1974) 'Provided versus elicited constructs: an explanation of Warr and Coffman's (1970) anomalous finding', *Brit. J. soc. clin. Psychol.*, *13*, 329
——, (1976) 'Does construing people as similar involve similar behaviour towards them? A subjective and objective replication', *Brit. J. soc. clin. Psychol.*, *15*, 93-5
BERNSTEIN, B. (1959) 'A public language: some sociological implications of a linguistic form', *Brit. J. Sociol.*, *10*, 311-26
——, (1961) 'Social class and linguistic development: a theory of social learning' in A. H. Hasley, J. Floud and A. C. Anderson (eds.), *Economy, Education and Society*, Free Press
BEVERIDGE, M. (1982) 'Classroom constructs: an interpretative approach to young children's language' in M. Beveridge (ed.), *Children's thinking through language*, E. Arnold, London
BIERI, J. (1955) 'Cognitive complexity-simplicity and predictive behavior, *J. abnorm. soc. Psychol.*, *51*, 263-8
——, ATKINS, A. L. BRIAR, S., LEADMAN, R. L., MILLER, H. and TRIPODI, T. (1966) *Clinical and Social Judgment: the discrimination of behavioural information*, Wiley
BIJOU, S. W. and BAEUR, D. M. (1966) 'Operant methods in child behavior and development' in W. K. Honig (ed.), *Operant Behavior: Areas of Research and Application*, Appleton-Century-Crofts, New York
BONARIUS, J. C. J. (1965) 'Research in the personal construct theory of George A. Kelly' in B. A. Maher (ed.), *Progress in Experimental Personality Research*, vol. 2, Academic Press
——, (1970) 'Fixed role therapy: a double paradox, *Brit. J. med. Psychol.*, *43*, 213-19
——, (1971) *Personal Construct Psychology and Extreme Response Style*, Swets and Zeitlinger, N. V.
——, HOLLAND, R. and ROSENBERG, S. (eds.) *Recent Advances in the Theory and Practice of Personal Construct Psychology*, Macmillan, London (in press)
BORGATTA, E. F. and BALES, R. F. (1953), 'Interaction of individuals in reconstituted groups', *Sociometry*, *16*, 327-38
BORING, E. G. (1929) 'The psychology of controversy', *Psychol. Rev.*, *36*, 97-121
——, (1950) *History of Experimental Psychology*, 2nd edn, Appleton-Century-Crofts, New York
BOXER, P. J. (1980) 'Supporting a reflexive theory of form', *Human Relations* (in press)
——, (1981) 'Supporting reflective learning: towards a reflexive theory of form' in H. Bonarius, R. Holland and S. Rosenberg (eds.), *Personal Construct Psychology: Recent Advances in Theory and Practice*, Macmillan, London
BRIERLEY, D. W. (1967) 'The use of personality constructs by children of three different ages', unpublished Ph.D. thesis, London University
BROVERMAN, I., VOGEL, S., BROVERMAN, D., CLARKSON, F. and ROSENKRANTZ, P. (1972) 'Sex-role stereotypes: a current appraisal', *J. soc. Issues*, *28*, 59-78
BRUNER, J. S. (1956) 'You are your constructs', *Contemp. Psychol.*, *1*, 355-7

BURGESS, R. (1968) 'Communication networks: an experimental re-evaluation', *J. exp. soc. Psychol.*, *4*, 324-37

BUTTON, E. (1980) *Construing and Clinical Outcome in Anorexia Nervosa*, unpublished Ph.D. thesis, University of London

——, (1983) 'Construing the anorexic' in J. Adams-Webber and J. Mancuso (eds.), *Applications of Personal Construct Theory*, Academic Press, Toronto

——, (1985) *Personal Construct Theory and Mental Health*, Croom Helm, London

CAINE, T. M. and SMAIL, D. J. (1969) *The Treatment of Mental Illness: Science, Faith and the Therapeutic Personality*, University of London Press

CAINE, T. M. and SMAIL, D. J. (1969a) 'The effects of personality and training on attitudes to treatment: preliminary investigations', *Brit. J. med. Psychol.*, *42*, 277-82

CANTER, D. (1970) 'Individual response to the physical environment', *Bull. Brit. Psychol. Soc.* (abstract), *23*, 123

CAPLAN, H. L., RHODE, P. D., SHAPIRO, D. A. and WATSON, J. P. (1974) 'Some correlates of repertory grid measures to study a Psychotherapeutic group', *Brit. J. med. Psychol.*, *48*, 217-26

CARTWRIGHT, R. D. and LERNER, B. (1963) 'Empathy, need to change and improvement with psychotherapy, *J. Consult. Psychol.*, *27*, 138-44

CHAMBERS, W. and SANDERS, J. (1984) 'Alcoholism and logical consistency of personal constructs', *Psychological Reports*, *54*, 882

CHAPANIS, N. P. and CHAPANIS, A. (1964) 'Cognitive dissonance: five years later', *Psychol. Bull.*, *61*, 1-22

CLARKE, A. D. B., CLARKE, A. M. and REIMAN, S. (1958) 'Cognitive and social changes in the feeble-minded - three further studies', *Brit. J. Psychol.*, *49*, 144-57

COCHRAN, L. (1976) 'Categorization and change in conceptual relatedness', *Can. J. Behav. Sci.*, *8*, 275-86

COX, C. B. and DYSON, A. E. (1969) *Fight for Education: A Black Paper*, Critical Quarterly Society

CROCKETT, W. H. and MEISEL, P. (1974) 'Construct connectedness, strength of disconfirmation, and impression change, *J. Person.*, *42*, 290-9

DAVIS, H. (1978) unpublished manuscript

——, (1979) 'An Exploration of Possible Relationships Between Construing and Behaviour in Mothers', unpublished Ph.D. thesis, University of London

DAWES, A. (1985) 'Drug dependence' in E. Button (ed.), *Personal Construct Theory in Mental Health*, Croom Helm, London

DEUTSCH, M. and COLLINS, M. (1951) *Interracial Housing: A Psychological Evaluation of a Social Experiment*, University of Minnesota Press

DUCK, S. W. (1973), *Personal Relationships and Personal Constructs*, Wiley

——, (1979), 'The personal and the interpersonal in personal construct theory in P. Stringer and D. Bannister (eds.), *Constructs of Sociality and Individuality*, Academic Press

——, (1983), 'Sociality and cognition in personal construct theory' in J. Adams-Webber and J. Mancuso (eds.), *Applications of Personal Construct Theory*, Academic Press

——, and SPENCER, C. (1972) 'Personal constructs and friendship formation', *J. person. soc. Psychol.*, *23*, 40-5

DU MAS, F. M. (1955) 'Science and the single case', *Psychol. Reps.*, *1*, 65-75

DU PREEZ, P. (1972), 'The construction of alternatives in parliamentary debate: a psychological theory and political analysis', *S. Afric. J. Psychol.*, *2*, 23-40

——, (1979) 'The politics of identity' in P. Stringer and D. Bannister (eds.), *Constructs of Sociality and Individuality*, Academic Press

——, (1980) *The Politics of Identity: Ideology and the Human Image*, Blackwell, Oxford

EARL, P. (1983) *The Economic Imagination*, Sharpe, New York

EDEN, C., JONES, S. and SIMS, D. (1979) *Thinking in Organizations*, Macmillan, London

ELLIS, A. and GRIEGER, R. (1977) *Handbook of Rational-Emotive Therapy*, Springer, New York

EPTING, F. (1984) *Personal Construct Counselling and Psychotherapy*, Wiley, New York

EVESHAM, M. and FRANSELLA, F. *Journal of Communication Disorders* (in press)

FESTINGER, L. (1957) *A Theory of Cognitive Dissonance*, Stanford University Press

FIELDING, J. M. (1975) 'A technique for measuring outcome in group psychotherapy', *Brit. J. med. Psychol.*, *48*, 189-98

FRANSELLA, F. (1965) 'The effects of imposed rhythm and certain aspects of personality on the speech of stutterers', unpublished Ph.D. thesis, London University

——, (1968) 'Self concepts and the stutterer', *Brit. J. Psychiat.*, *114*, 1531-5

——, (1969) 'The stutterer as subject or object?', in B. B. Gray and G. England (eds.), *Stuttering and the Conditioning Therapies*, Monterey Institute of Speech & Hearing, California

——, (1970) '. . . And then there was one' in D. Bannister (ed.), *Perspectives in Personal Construct Theory*, Academic Press

——, (1972) *Personal Change and Reconstruction: research on a treatment of stuttering*, Academic Press

——, (1974) 'Thinking and the obsessional' in H. R. Beech (ed.), *Obsessional States*, Methuen, London

——, (1975) *Need to Change?*, Methuen, London

——, (1977) 'The self and the stereotype' in D. Bannister (ed.), *New Perspectives in Personal Construct Theory*, Academic Press

——, (ed.) (1978) *Personal Construct Psychology 1977*, Academic Press,

——, (1980) 'Nature babbling to herself: the self characterization as a therapeutic tool' in J. G. J. Bonarius and S. Rosenberg (eds.), *Recent Advances in the Theory and Practice of Personal Construct Psychology*, Macmillan, London (in press)

——, (1982) 'Personal meanings and personal constructs' in E. Shepherd and J. P. Watson (eds.), *Personal Meanings*, Wiley

——, (1983) 'What sort of scientist is the person-as-scientist' in J. Adams-Webber and J. Mancuso (eds.), *Applications of Personal Construct Theory*, Academic Press, London

——, (1983a) 'Threat and the scientist' in G. M. Breakwell (ed.), *Threatened Identities*, Wiley

——, (1985) 'Resistance: a personal construct view', *British Journal of Cognitive Psychotherapry* (in press)

——, (1985a) 'Individual psychotherapy' in E. Button (ed.), *Personal Construct Theory and Mental Health*, Croom Helm, London

——, (1985b) 'Personal construct therapy' in W. Dryden (ed.), *Individual Therapy in Britain*, Harper & Row, London

——, and ADAMS, B. (1966) 'An illustration of the use of repertory grid technique in a clinical setting', *Brit. J. soc. clin. Psychol.*, *5*, 51-62

——, and BANNISTER, D. (1967) 'A validation of repertory grid technique as a measure of political construing', *Acta Psychol.*, *26*, 97-106

——, and BANNISTER, D. (1977) *A Manual of Repertory Grid Technique*, Academic Press

——, and BUTTON, E. (1984) 'The "construing" of self and body size in relation to the maintenance of weight gain in anorexia nervosa' in P. L. Darby (ed.), *Anorexia Nervosa: Recent Developments in Research*, Alan R. Liss, New York

——, and CRISP, A. H. (1971) 'Conceptual organization and weight change' in R. A. Pierloot (ed.), *Recent Research in Psychosomatics*, S. Karger, Basel

——, and FROST, K. (1977) *On Being a Woman*, Tavistock, London

——, and JOYSTON-BECHAL, M. P. (1971) 'An investigation of conceptual process and pattern change in a psychotherapy group', *Brit. J. Psychiat.*, *119*, 199-206

FÜRST, H. (1978) *Modes of constructions and their change through validation and invalidation*, Acta Universitatis Upsaliensis, vol. 5, Uppsala

GARDNER, H. (1977) *The Shattered Mind: the person after brain damage*, Routledge and Kegan Paul, London

GEIWITZ, P. J. (1969) *Non-Freudian Personality Theories*, Brooks-Cole

GILLARD, D. (1982) 'How to explain history', *Constructs*, *1*, 3

——, (1984) 'British and Russian relations with Asian governments in the nineteenth century' in H. Bull and A. Watson (eds.), *The Expansion of International Society*, Clarendon Press, Oxford

GOLD, M. (1969) 'Juvenile delinquency as a symptom of alienation', *J. soc. Issues*, *25*, 121-35

GORDON, A. (1977) 'Thinking with restricted language: A personal construct investigation of pre-lingually profoundly deaf apprentices', *Brit. J. Psychol.*, *68*, 253-5

GREENBERG, L. S. and SAFRAN, J. D. (1984) 'Integrating affect and cognition: a perspective on the process of therapeutic change', *Cognitive Therapy and Research*, *8*, 559-78

HALL, C. S. and LINDZEY, G. (1957) *Theories of Personality*, Wiley

HALL, M. F. (1966) 'The generality of cognitive complexity — simplicity', unpublished Ph.D. thesis, Vanderbilt University

HAMILTON, D. L. (1968) 'Personality attributes associated with extreme response style', *Psychol. Bull.*, *69*, 192-203

HARGREAVES, D. H. (1977) 'The process of typification in classroom interaction: models and methods', *Brit. J. educ. Psychol.*, *47*, 274-84

HAYDEN, B. and NASBY, W. (1977) 'Interpersonal conceptual structures, predictive accuracy, and social adjustment of emotionally disturbed boys', *J. abn. Psychol.*, *86*, 315-20

HEATHER, N. (1979) 'The structure of delinquent values: a repertory grid study', *Brit. J. soc. clin. Psychol.*, *18*, 263-75

HINKLE, D. (1965) 'The change of personal constructs from the viewpoint of a theory of construct implications', unpublished Ph.D. thesis, Ohio State University

HOFFMAN, D. T., SCHACKNER, R. and GOLDBLATT, R. (1970) 'Friendliness of the experimenter', *Psychol. Rec.*, *20*, 41-4

HOGAN, R. (1976) *Personality Theory: The Personological Tradition*, Prentice-Hall, New Jersey

HOLLAND, R. (1970) 'George Kelly: constructive innocent and reluctant existentialist' in D. Bannister (ed.), *Perspectives in Personal Construct Theory*, Academic Press

HOLLAND, S. (1971) 'Perceived powerlessness of self and others among delinquents', unpublished Master's thesis, London University

HONESS, T. (1976) 'Cognitive complexity and social prediction', *Brit. J. soc. clin. Psychol.*, *15*, 23-31

——, (1977), 'An implication grid suitable for use in developmental research, unpublished manuscript

——, (1978) 'A comparison of the implication and repertory grid techniques', *Brit. J. Psychol.*, *69*, 305-12

——, (1979) 'Children's implicit theories of their peers: a developmental analysis', *Brit. J. Psychol.*, *70*, 417-24

HONIKMAN, B. (1976) 'Construct theory as an approach to architectural and environmental design' in P. Slater (ed.), *Explorations of Intrapersonal Space*, vol. 1, Wiley

HOWARD, J. W. (1970) 'Management - power and independence', unpublished manuscript

HOY, R. M. (1973) 'The meaning of alcoholism for alcoholics: a repertory grid study', *Brit. J. soc. clin. Psychol.*, *12*, 98-9

HUDSON, L. (1968) *Contrary Imaginations*, Penguin Books, Harmondsworth

——, (1970) *Frames of Mind*, Penguin Books, Harmondsworth

HUMPHREY, G. (1933) *The Nature of Learning*, Harcourt, Brace & World

HUMPHRIS, M. (1977) 'An evaluation, using Kelly's repertory grid technique, of the self-image of boys, construed by their teachers as having speech and/or language difficulties', unpublished M.Sc. dissertation, London University

JACKSON, S. R. and BANNISTER, D. (1985) 'Growing into self' in D. Bannister (ed.), *Issues and Approaches in Personal Construct Theory*, Academic Press, London

JAMES, W. (1892) *Psychology: The Briefer Course*, Holt

JENSEN, A. R. (1972) *Genetics and Education*, Harper & Row

JOHNSON, W. (1942) 'A study of the onset and development of stuttering', *J. Speech Dis.*, 7, 251-7

JONES, H. (1985) 'Creativity and depression: an idiographic study' in A. W. Landfield and F. Epting (eds.), *Applications of Personal Construct Psychology*, University of Nebraska Press, Lincoln

KARST, T. O. and GROUTT, J. W. (1977) 'Inside mystical minds, in D. Bannister (ed.), *New Perspectives in Personal Construct Theory*, Academic Press

KARST, T. O. and TREXLER, L. D. (1970) 'Initial study using fixed-role and rational-emotive therapy in treating public-speaking anxiety', *J. consult. clin. Psychol.*, *34*, 360-6

KELLEY, H. H. (1950) 'The warm-cold variable in first impressions', *J. Person.*, *18*, 431-9

KELLY, G. A. (1930) 'The social inheritance in P. Stringer and D. Bannister (eds.), *Constructs of Sociality and Individuality*, Academic Press (1979)

——, (1955) *The Psychology of Personal Constructs*, vols. 1 and 2, Norton

——, (1961) 'The abstraction of human processes', *Proceedings of the Fourteenth International Congress of Applied Psychology*, Munksgaard, Copenhagen

——, (1961a) 'Suicide: the personal construct point of view', in N. L. Farberow and E. S. Schneidman (eds.), *The Cry for Help*, McGraw-Hill

——, (1962) 'Europe's matrix of decision' in M. R. Jones (ed.), *Nebraska Symposium on Motivation*, University of Nebraska Press, Lincoln

——,, (1966) transcript of a tape-recorded conversation with F. Fransella

——, (1969) 'Man's construction of his alternatives' in B. Maher (ed.), *Clinical Psychology and Personality: Selected Papers of George Kelly*, Wiley

——, (1969a) 'Humanistic methodology in psychological research' in B. Maher (ed.), *Clinical Psychology and Personality: Selected Papers of George Kelly*, Wiley

——, (1969b) 'Ontological acceleration' in B. A. Maher (ed.), *Clinical Psychology and Personality: Selected Papers of George Kelly*, Wiley

——, (1969c) 'The strategy of psychological research in B. A. Maher (ed.), *Clinical Psychology and Personality: Selected Papers of George Kelly*, Wiley

——, (1969d) 'Personal construct theory and the psychotherapeutic interview' in B. A. Maher (ed.), *Clinical Psychology and Personality: Selected Papers of George Kelly*, Wiley

——, (1969e) 'Hostility in B. A. Maher (ed.), *Clinical Psychology and Personality: Selected Papers of George Kelly*, Wiley

——, (1969f) 'Pyschotherapy and the nature of man' in B. A. Maher (ed.), *Clinical Psychology and Personality: Selected Papers of George Kelly*, Wiley

——, (1970) 'A brief introduction to personal construct theory' in D. Bannister (ed.), *Perspectives in Personal Construct Theory*, Academic Press

——, (1970a) 'Behaviour is an experiment' in D. Bannister (ed.), *Perspectives in Personal Construct Theory*, Academic Press

——, (1977) 'The psychology of the unknown' in D. Bannister (ed.), *New Perspectives in Personal Construct Theory*, Academic Press

——, (1978) 'Confusion and the clock' in F. Fransella (ed.), *Personal Construct Psychology, 1977*, Academic Press, London

——, (1979) 'Social inheritance' in P. Stringer and D. Bannister (eds.), *Constructs of Sociality and Individuality*, Academic Press

——, (1980) 'A psychology of the optimal man in A. W. Landfield and L. M. Leitner (eds.), *Personal Construct Psychology: Psychotherapy and Personality*, Wiley, New York

KRIEGER, S. R., EPTING, F. R. and LEITNER, L. M. (1974) 'Personal constructs, threat and attitudes to death', *Omega*, 5, 299-310

KRECH, D., CRUTCHFIELD, R. S. and BALLACHEY, E. L. (1962) *Individual in Society: A Textbook of Social Psychology*, McGraw-Hill

KRECHEVSKY, I. (1932) 'Hypotheses in rats', *Psychol. Rev.*, 39, 516-32

KUUSINEN, J. and NYSTEDT, L. (1975a) 'Individual versus provided constructs, cognitive complexity and extremity of ratings in person perception', *Scand. J. Psychol.*, 16, 137-48

LAING, R. D. and ESTERSON, A. (1964) *Sanity, Madness and the Family*, Tavistock, London

LANDFIELD, A. W. (1968) 'The extremity rating revisited within the context of personal construct theory' *Brit. J. soc. clin. Psychol.*, 7, 135-9

——, (1971) *Personal Construct Systems in Psychotherapy*, Rand McNally

——, (1976) 'A personal construct approach to suicidal behaviour' in P. Slater (ed.), *Explorations of Intrapersonal Space*, vol. 1, Wiley

——, (1977) (ed.) *Nebraska Symposium on Motivation 1976*, University of Nebraska Press, Lincoln

——, and LEITNER, L. M. (1980) *Personal Construct Psychology: Psychotherapy and Personality*, Wiley, New York

LEAVITT, H. J. (1951) 'Some effects of certain communication patterns on group performance', *J. abn. soc. Psychol.*, 46, 38-50

LEMAN, G. (1970) 'Words and worlds' in D. Bannister (ed.), *Perspectives in Personal Construct Theory*, Academic Press

——, (1971) personal communication

LEMON, N. (1975) 'Linguistic development and conceptualization: a bilingual study', *J. cross-cult. Psychol*, 6, 173-88

LESTER. D. (1968) 'Attempted suicide as a hostile act', *J. Psychol.*, 68, 243-8

——, (1969) 'Resentment and dependency in the suicidal individual', *J. gen. Psychol.*, 81, 137-45

LEVINE, S. (1956) 'A further study of infantile handling and adult avoidance learning', *J. Person*, 25, 70-80

LEVY, L. H. (1956) 'Personal constructs and predictive behaviour', *J. abn. soc. Psychol.*, 53, 54-8

LIDZ, T. (1964) *The Family and Human Adaptation*, Hogarth

LITTLE, B. R. (1968) 'Factors affecting the use of psychological v. non-psychological constructs on the Rep Test'., *Bull. Brit. Psychol. Soc.*, 21,70, 34

LOCK, A. (1976) 'Acts not sentences' in W. von Raffler-Engel and Y. Lebrun (eds.), *Baby Talk and Infant Speech*, Swets Zeitlinger, N. V.

McCOMISKY, J. *et al* (1969) 'An experimental investigation of some basic concepts in architecture', *Int. J. educ. Sci.*, 3, 199-208

McCOY, M. (1977) 'A reconstruction of emotion' in D. Bannister (ed.), *New Perspectives in Personal Construct Theory*, Academic Press

McFALL, R. M. (1965) personal communication

McPHERSON, F. M., ARMSTRONG, J. and HEATHER, B. B. (1975) 'Psychological construing, difficulty and thought disorder', *Brit. J. med. Psychol.*, *48*, 303-15

McPHERSON, F. M., BLACKBURN, I. M., DRAFFAN, J. W. and McFADYEN, M. (1973) 'A further study of the grid test of thought disorder', *Brit. J. soc. clin. Psychol.*, *12*, 420-7

McPHERSON, F. M. and WALTON, H. J. (1970) 'The dimensions of psychotherapy group interaction: an analysis of clinicians' constructs', *Brit. J. med. Psychol.*, *43*, 281-90

MAIR, J. M. M. (1964) 'The derivation, reliability and validity of grid measures: some problems and suggestions', *Bull. Brit. Psychol. Soc.*, *17*, 55, 7A

——, (1964a) 'The concepts of reliability and validity in relation to construct theory and repertory grid technique' in N. Warren (ed.), *Brunel Construct Theory Seminar Report*, Brunel University

——, (1967) 'Some problems of repertory grid measurement. 2: The use of whole-figure constructs', *Brit. J. Psychol.*, *58*, 271-82

——, (1970) 'Experimenting with individuals', *Brit. J. med. Psychol.*, *43*, 245-56

——, (1970a) 'Psychologists are human too' in D. Bannister (ed.), *Perspectives in Personal Construct Theory*, Academic Press

——, (1977) 'The community of self' in D. Bannister (ed.), *New Perspectives in Personal Construct Theory*, Academic Press

——, (1977a) 'Metaphors for living' in A. W. Landfield (ed.), *Nebraska Symposium on Motivation 1976*, University of Nebraska Press, Lincoln

MAKHLOUF-NORRIS, F., JONES, G. and NORRIS, H. (1970) 'Articulation of the conceptual structure in obsessional neurosis, *Brit. J. soc. clin. Psychol.*, *9*, 264-74

MANCUSO, J. C. (1979) 'Reprimand: the construing of the rule violator's construct system' in P. Stringer and D. Bannister (eds.), *Constructs of Sociality and Individuality*, Academic Press

——, and ADAMS-WEBBER, J. (eds.) (1982), *The Construing Person*, Praeger, New York

——, and HUNTER, K. V. (1983) 'Anticipation, motivation or emotion' in J. Adams-Webber and J. Mancuso (eds.), *Applications of Personal Construct Theory*, Academic Press, London

MARCEIL, J. C. (1977) 'Implicit dimensions of idiography and nomothesis: a reformulation', *Amer. Psychol.*, *32*, 1046-55

MEICHENBAUM, D. (1977) *Cognitive-Behaviour Modification: an Integrative Approach*, Plenum Press, New York

MESHOULAM, U. (1978) 'There is more to stuttering than meets the ear: stutterers' construing of speaking situations' in F. Fransella (ed.), *Personal Construct Psychology 1977*, Academic Press

MICKLEM, S. (1978), 'Silence in the classroom' unpublished M.Sc. dissertation, London University

MILGRAM, S. (1974) *Obedience to Authority, an experimental view*, Harper Row

MILLER, K. and TREACHER, A. (1981) 'Delinquency: a personal construct approach' in H. Bonarius, R. Holland, and S. Rosenberg, (eds.), *Personal Construct Psychology: Recent Advances in Theory and Practice*, Macmillan, London

MISCHEL, W. (1980) 'George Kelly's anticipation of psychology: a personal tribute' in M. J. Mahoney (ed.), *Psychotherapy Process: current issues and future directions*, Plenum Press, New York

MIXON, D. (1972) 'Instead of deception', *J. theory. soc. Behav.*, *2*, 145-77

MORRIS, J. B. (1977) 'Towards a Personal Science' in D. Bannister (ed.), *New Perspectives in Personal Construct Theory*, Academic Press

——, (1977a) 'The prediction and measurement of change in a psychotherapy group using the repertory grid' in F. Fransella and D. Bannister (eds.), *A Manual for Repertory Grid Technique*, Academic Press

MOSCOVICI, S. (1976) *Social Influence and Social Change*, Academic Press

Moss, A. E. (1974) 'Hamlet and role construct theory', *Brit. J. med. Psychol.*, *43*, 253-64

Mueller, W. S. (1974) 'Cognitive complexity and salience of dimensions in person perception', *Austr. J. Psychol.*, *26*, 173-82

Nash, R. (1973) *Classrooms Observed*, Routledge and Kegan Paul, London

—, (1976) *Teacher Expectations and Pupil Learning*, Routledge and Kegan Paul, London

Neimeyer, R. A. (1984) 'Toward a personal construct conceptualization of depression and suicide' in F. R. Epting and R. A. Neimeyer (eds.), *Personal Meanings of Death: Applications of Personal Construct Theory in Clinical Practice*, Hemisphere/McGraw-Hill, New York

—, (1985) 'Personal construct therapy' in W. Dryden and W. Golden (eds.), *Cognitive and Behavioral Approaches to Psychotherapy*, Harper & Row, London

—, (1985a) 'Personal constructs in clinical practice in P. C. Kendall (ed.), *Advances in Cognitive-Behavioral Research and Therapy*, vol. 4, Academic Press, New York

—, (1985b) 'Personal constructs in depression: research and clinical implications' in E. Button (ed.), *Personal Construct Theory and Mental Health*, Croom Helm, London

—, (1985) *The Development of Personal Construct Psychology*, Nebraska University Press, Lincoln

—, Heath, A. E. and Strauss, J. (1985) 'Personal reconstruction during group cognitive therapy for depression' in F. R. Epting and A. W. Landfield (eds.), *Anticipating Personal Construct Theory*, Nebraska University Press, Lincoln

—, Klein, M. H., Gurman, A. F. and Greist, J. H. (1983) 'Cognitive structure and depressive symptomatology', *Brit. J. Psychother.*, *1*, 65-73

Norris, M. (1977) 'Construing in a detention centre' in D. Bannister (ed.), *New Perspectives in Personal Construct Theory*, Academic Press

Norris, H. and Makhlouf-Norris, F. (1976) 'The measurement of self-identity' in P. Slater (ed.), *Explorations of Intrapersonal Space*, Wiley

Notcutt, B. (1953) *The Psychology of Personality*, Methuen, London

O'Hare, D. P. A. and Gordon, I. E. (1976) 'An application of repertory grid technique to aesthetic measurement', *Percept. Motor Skills*, *42*, 1183-92

O'Reilly, J. (1977) 'The interplay between mothers and their children: a construct theory viewpoint' in D. Bannister (ed.), *New Perspectives in Personal Construct Theory*, Academic Press

O'Sullivan, B. (1985) 'Understanding the Experience of Agoraphobia', unpub. Ph.D. thesis, University of London

Orley, J. (1976) 'The use of grid technique in social anthropology' in P. Slater (ed.), *Explorations of Intrapersonal Space*, vol. 1: *The Measurement of Intrapersonal Space by Grid Technique*, Wiley

Orne, M. T. (1959) 'The nature of hypnosis: artifact and essence', *J. abn. soc. Psychol.*, *58*, 277-99

—, (1962) 'On the social psychology of the psychological experiment: with particular reference to demand characteristics and their implications', *Amer. Psychol.*, *17*, 776-83

Osgood, C. E., Suci, G. J. and Tannenbaum, P. M. (1957) *The Measurement of Meaning*, University of Illinois Press

Pervin, L. A. (1975) *Personality: Theory, Assessment and Research*, 2nd edn., Wiley

Piaget, J. (1977) *The Grasp of Consciousness: Action and Concept in the Young Child*, translation S. Wedgwood, Routledge and Kegan Paul, London

Pierce, A. H. (1908) 'The subconscious again', *J. Phil. Psychol. Sci. Meth.*, *5*, 264-71

Pope, M. (1978) 'Monitoring and reflecting in teacher training' in F. Fransella (ed.), *Personal Construct Psychology 1977*, Academic Press

——, and KEEN, T. (1981) *Personal Construct Psychology and Education*, Academic Press

POPPER, K. R. (1959) *The Logic of Scientific Discovery*, Hutchinson, London

PROCTOR, H. G. (1978) 'Personal construct theory and the family: a theoretical and methodological study', unpublished Ph.D. thesis, Bristol University

——, and PARRY, G. (1978) 'Constraint and freedom: the social origin of personal constructs' in F. Fransella (ed.), *Personal Construct Psychology 1977*, Academic Press

RADLEY, A. R. (1974) 'The effect of role enactment upon construed alternatives', *Brit. J. med. Psychol.*, 47, 313-20

——, (1978) 'The opposing self' in F. Fransella (ed.), *Personal Construct Psychology 1977*, Academic Press

RATHOD, P. (1983) 'Metaphors for the constuction of interpersonal relationships' in J. Adams-webber and J. Mancuso (eds.), *Applications of Personal Construct Theory*, Academic Press, Toronto

RAVENETTE, A. T. (1968) *Dimensions of Reading Difficulties*, Pergamon Press, Oxford

——, (1977) 'Personal construct theory: an approach to the psychological investigation of children and young people' in D. Bannister (ed.), *New Perspectives in Personal Construct Theory*, Academic Press

——, (1980) 'The exploration of consciousness: personal construct intervention with children' in *Personal Construct Psychology: Psychotherapy and Personality*, Wiley

REASON, P. and ROWAN, J. (eds.) (1981) *Human Inquiry*, Wiley, Chichester

REKER, G. T. (1974) 'Interpersonal conceptual structures of emotionally disturbed and normal boys', *J. abn. Psychol.*, 83, 380-6

RIGDON, N. A. and EPTING, F. R. (1983) 'A personal construct perspective on an obsessive client in J. Adams-Webber and J. Mancuso (eds.), *Applications of Personal Construct Theory*, Academic Press, New York

RILEY, S. and PALMER, J. (1976) 'Of attitudes and latitudes: a repertory grid study of perceptions of seaside resorts' in P. Slater (ed.), *Explorations of Intrapersonal Space*, vol. 1, Wiley

ROGERS, C. A. (1958) 'A process conception of psychotherapy', *Amer. Psychol.*, 13, 142-9

ROLLIN, H. R. (1969) *The Mentally Abnormal Offender and the Law*, Pergamon Press, Oxford

ROSEN, H. (1972) *Language and Class: a critical look at the theories of Basil Bernstein*, Falling Wall Press

ROSENTHAL, R. (1967) 'Covert communication in the psychological experiment', *Psychol. Bull.*, 67, 356-67

ROSIE, A. J. (1979) 'Teachers and children: interpersonal relations and the classroom' in P. Stringer and D. Bannister (eds.) *Constructs of Sociality and Individuality*, Academic Press

ROWE, D. (1971) 'Poor prognosis in a case of depression as predicted by the repertory grid', *Brit. J. Psychiat.*, 118, 297-300

——, (1978), *The Experience of Depression*, Wiley

——, (1983) *Depression: The Way Out of Your Prison*, Routledge and Kegan Paul, London

RUNKEL, P. J. and DAMRIN, D. E. (1961) 'Effect of training and anxiety upon teachers' preference for information about students', *J. educ. Psychol.*, 52, 345-61

RYCHLAK, J. F. (1968) *A Philosophy of Science for Personality Theory*, Houghton Mifflin

RYLE, A. and BREEN, D. (1972) 'Some differences in the personal constructs of neurotic and normal subjects', *Brit. J. Psychiat.*, 120, 483-9

RYLE, A. and LIPSHITZ, S. (1975) 'Recording change in marital therapy with the reconstruction grid', *Brit. J. med. Psychol.*, 48, 39-48

RYLE, A. and LUNGHI, M. E. (1969) 'The measurement of relevant change after psychotherapy: use of repertory grid testing', *Brit. J. Psychiat.*, *115*, 1297-1304

RYLE, A. and LUNGHI, M. E. (1970) 'The dyad grid: a modification of repertory grid technique', *Brit. J. Psychiat.*, *117*, 323-7

SALMON, P. (1963) 'A clinical investigation of sexual identity', unpublished case study

——, (1969) 'Differential conforming as a developmental process', *Brit. J. soc. clin. Psychol.*, *8*, 22-31

——, (1970) 'A psychology of personal growth' in D. Bannister (ed.), *Perspectives in Personal Construct Theory*, Academic Press

——, (1978) 'Doing psychological research in F. Fransella (ed.), *Personal Construct Psychology 1977*, Academic Press,

——, (1979) 'Children as social beings' in P. Stringer and D. Bannister (eds.), *Constructs of Sociality and Individuality*, Academic Press

——, and CLAIRE, H. (1984) *Classroom Collaboration*, Routledge and Kegan Paul, London

SALMON, P., BRAMLEY, J. and PRESLY, A. S. (1967) 'The word-in-context test as a measure of conceptualization in schizophrenics with and without thought disorder', *Brit. J. med. Psychol.*, *40*, 253-9

SECHREST, L. B. (1963) 'The psychology of personal constructs: George Kelly' in J. M. Wepman and R. W. Heine (eds.), *Concepts of Personality*, Aldine

SHEEHAN, M. J. (1981) 'Constructs and conflict in depression', *Brit. J. Psychol.*, *72*, 197-209

——, (1983) 'Personal Construct Psychotherapy and Depresson', unpub. Ph.D. thesis, University of London

SHOTTER, J. (1974) 'The development of personal powers' in M. P. M. Richards (ed.), *The Integration of the Child into a Social World*, Cambridge University Press

SKENE, R. A. (1973) 'Construct shift in the treatment of a case of homosexuality', *Brit. J. med. Psychol.*, *46*, 287-92

SKODAK, M. and SKEELS, H. M. (1949) 'A final follow-up study of one hundred adopted children', *J. genet. Psychol.*, *75*, 85-125

SLATER, P. (ed.) (1976) *The Measurement of Intrapersonal Space by Grid Technique* vol. 1, *Explorations of Intrapersonal Space*, Wiley

——, (1977), *The Measurement of Intrapersonal Space by Grid Technique* vol. 2, *Dimensions of Intrapersonal Space*, Wiley

SMAIL, D. J. (1970) 'Neurotic symptoms, personality and personal constructs', *Brit. J. Psychiat.*, *117*, 645-8

STEFAN, C. (1977) 'Core role theory and implications' in D. Bannister (ed.), *New Perspectives in Personal Construct Theory*, Academic Press

——, and LINDER, H. B. (1985), 'Suicide: an experience of chaos or fatalism?' in D. Bannister (ed.), *Issues and Approaches in Personal Construct Theory*, Academic Press, London

STRACHAN, A. and JONES, D. (1982) 'Changes in identification during adolescence: a personal construct theory approach', *J. Person. Assess.*, *46*, 529-35

STRINGER, P. (1976) 'Repertory grids in the study of environmental perceptions of seaside resorts' in P. Slater (ed.), *Explorations of Intrapersonal Space*, Wiley

STRINGER P. and BANNISTER, D. (1979) (eds.) *Constructs of Sociality and Individuality*, Academic Press

THOMAS, L. F. (1978) 'A personal construct approach to learning in education, training and therapy' in F. Fransella (ed.), *Personal Construct Psychology 1977*, Academic Press

THOMAS, L. F. and HARRI-AUGSTEIN, E. S. (1983) 'The self-organized learner as personal scientist: a conversational technology for reflecting on behavior and experience' in J. Adams-Webber and J. Mancuso (eds.), *Applications of Personal Construct Theory*, Academic Press, Toronto

THOMAS, L. F. and HARRI-AUGSTEIN, E. S. (1985) *Self-organised Learning*, Routledge and Kegan Paul, London

TODD, N. (1977) 'Religious belief and personal construct theory', unpublished Ph.D. thesis, Nottingham University

TOLMAN, E. C. (1932) *Purposive Behavior in Animals and Man*, Appleton-Century-Crofts, New York

TROWER, P., BRYANT, B. and ARGYLE, M. (1978) *Social Skills and Mental Health*, Methuen, London

TRYON, R. C. (1934) 'Individual differences' in F. A. Moss (ed.), *Comparative Psychology*, Prentice-Hall, New Jersey

TSCHUDI, F. (1977) 'Loaded and honest questions' in D. Bannister (ed.), *New Perspectives in Personal Construct Theory*, Academic Press

VINCE, M. (1967) 'Respiration as a factor in communication between quail embryos', *Bull. Brit. Psychol,. Soc.*(abstract), *20*, 29A

WALKER, A. M., RABLEN, R. A., and ROGERS, C. A. (1960) 'Development of a scale to measure process changes in psychotherapy', *J. clin. Psychol.*, *16*, 79-85

WARR, P. B. and COFFMAN, T. L. (1970) 'Personality, involvement and extremity judgment', *Brit. J. soc. clin. Psychol.*, *9*, 108-21

WARREN, N. (1966) 'Social class and construct systems: examination of the cognitive structure of two social class groups', *Brit. J. soc. clin. Psychol.*, *4*, 254-63

WATSON, J. P. (1970) 'A repertory grid method of studying groups', *Brit. J.Psychiat.*, *117*, 309-18

WEINREICH, P. (1979) 'Ethnicity and adolescent identity conflicts' in V. Saifullah Kahn and D. Loudon (eds.), *Support and Stress: Minority Families in Britain*, Macmillan, London

——, (1980) A manual for identity exploration using personal constructs, Social Science Research Council, London

WHORF, B. L. (1956) in J. B. Carroll (ed.), *Language, Thought and Reality: Selected Writings of Benjamin Lee Whorf*, Wiley

WOLPE, J. (1954) 'Reciprocal inhibition as the main basis of psychotherapeutic effects', *Amer. Med. Assoc. Arch. Neurol. Psychiat.*, *72*, 205-26

WOOSTER, A. D. (1970) 'Formation of stable and discrete concepts of personality by normal and mentally retarded boys', *J. ment. Subnorm.*, *6*, 24-8

WRIGHT, K. J. T. (1970) 'Exploring the uniqueness of common complaints', *Brit. J. med. Psychol.*, *43*, 221-32

YORKE, D. M. (1983) 'Straight or bent? An inquiry into rating scales in repertory grids', *Brit. Educ. Res. J.*, *9*, 141-51

ZELHART, P. and JACKSON, T. (1983) 'George A. Kelly, 1931-1943: environmental influences on a developing theorist' in J. Adams-Webber and J. Mancuso (eds.), *Applications of Personal Construct Theory*, Academic Press

AUTHOR INDEX

Adams, B. 48, 66, 78, 138
Adams-Webber, J. R. 7, 34, 45, 52,
  66
Agnew, J. 73, 103, 143, 167
Allport, G. W. 41, 42, 43
Applebee, A. N. 72
Argyris, C. 131
Armstrong, J. 145
Asch, S. E. 93
Ashworth, C. M. 152

Bakan, D. 167
Baker, R. 44
Baillie-Brohman, R. 82
Bales, R. F. 102
Ballachey, E. L. 97
Baloff, N. 43
Bannister, D. 4, 12, 15, 16, 17, 21,
  30, 33, 34, 37, 39, 48, 49, 51, 54, 60,
  71, 73, 77, 81, 85, 96, 103, 106, 118,
  126, 129, 134, 136, 143, 144, 146,
  148, 150, 158, 162
Bartlett, F. C. 36
Barton, E. S. 83
Bateson, G. 148
Bauer, D. M. 114
Beail, N. 51
Beck, A. T. 115
Becker, S. W. 43
Beech, H. R. 121
Bender, M. P. 53, 108
Bernstein, B. 105, 106
Beveridge, M. 75
Bieri, J. 52, 106
Bijou, S. W. 114
Blackburn, I. M. 142, 152
Bonarius, J. C. J. 53, 120
Borgath, E. F. 102
Boring, E. G. 41
Bott, M. 126, 129
Boxer, P. J. 44
Bramley, J. 145
Breen, D. 56
Brierley, D. W. 71
Bruner, J. S. 21
Broverman, D. 99
Broverman, I. 99
Burgess, R. 101
Button, E. 118, 124

Caine, T. M. 136
Canter, D. 106
Caplan, H. L. 56, 132
Cartwright, R. D. 129
Chambers, W. 152
Chomsky, N. 102
Claire, H. 74, 75
Clarkson, F. 99
Cochran, L. 126
Copeman, T. L. 53
Collins, M. 98
Cox, C. B. 84
Crisp, A. H. 137
Crockett, W. H. 109
Crutchfield, R. S. 67

Damrin, D. G. 77
Davis, H. 69
Dawes, A. 152
Deutsch, M. 98
Duck, S. W. 109, 110
Du Mas, F. M. 42
Du Preez, P. 103, 136
Draffan, J. W. 142
Dyson, A. E. 84

Earl, P. 44
Ebbinghaus, R. 36
Eden, C. 44
Elgar, E. 86
Ellis, A. 115
Epting, F. 118, 120, 139, 152
Esterson, A. 148
Evesham, M. 124

Fielding, J. M. 132
Fransella, F. 48, 49, 50, 51, 54, 56, 60,
  64, 69, 72, 99, 100, 101, 118, 121,
  122, 124, 125, 130, 131, 137, 138, 143,
  150, 151, 159
Freud, S. 3, 7, 28, 44, 66, 68
Frost, K. 72, 100, 159
Furst, H. 77

Gardner, H. 38
Gillard, D. 44
Gold, M. 80
Goldblatt, R. 91
Gordon, A. 44, 82

189

190 *Index*

SUBJECT INDEX

193

194 *Index*